FIRST STEPS IN LATIN

FIRST STEPS
IN LATIN

BY

F. RITCHIE, M.A.

NEW EDITION REVISED BY

R. D. WORMALD, M.A.

LONGMANS

LONGMANS, GREEN AND CO LTD
48, Grosvenor Street, London W.1.
*Associated companies, branches and representatives
throughout the world*

New edition 1957
New impression 1966

PRINTED IN HONG KONG
BY DAI NIPPON PRINTING CO. (INTERNATIONAL) LTD.

PREFACE TO REVISED EDITION

THE changes made by Mr. J. W. Bartram in the New Edition (1939) of this well-known work were mostly typographical, though he also carried out the exacting task of marking vowel quantities (including 'hidden' quantities) in conformity with modern practice.

Since then several suggestions have been received from various quarters about improvements in detail; and it has now become practicable to incorporate them in a Revised Edition. Most of the alterations fall under three main headings:—

(1) Several new words have been introduced, either in the Special Vocabularies (*ager, periculum, cubile, vito, habeo, dormio, scio*) or in the General Vocabularies for use in the later Exercises (*Britannia, causa, femina, gladius, insula, lupus, piscis, pauci, quis, celo, paro*).

(2) Word-order in some of the Latin-English exercises has been amended.

(3) 'Thou,' 'Ye,' and other archaisms have been removed.

The opportunity has also been taken of correcting a few errors of Latinity, such as the use of *punior* in a passive sense, that were contained in the original version. But the book remains substantially as it was: and it is hoped that the improvements now made will commend themselves to old friends and gain new ones.

R. D. W.

1956

AUTHOR'S PREFACE

THE difficulty which inevitably surrounds the beginning of Latin by very young pupils is often unnecessarily increased by the common practice of separating the study of the Accidence from its practical application. Exercises in Translation and Composition, even of the most elementary kind, are too frequently postponed till the Declensions and Conjugations have been gone through, and the memory of the pupil being thus burdened with a mass of forms, the use and meaning of which are not yet apparent, inaccuracy and mental confusion are the result. An attempt has here been made to make the application run side by side with the study of the Accidence, and at the same time to introduce some of the simpler rules of Syntax. As each Declension or Tense is learned, the formation exhibited in the type is applied to other Nouns or Verbs, and sentences framed to illustrate the use of the inflexions, and the meaning of the Syntax rules.

With a view to avoiding or lessening the bewilderment usually produced upon the mind of a beginner by the use of a complete Grammar, everything not essential to the structure of a simple sentence has been carefully excluded. Thus, in the Conjugation of the Verbs the Indicative Mood only is introduced; irregularities of every kind have been, as far as possible, avoided, and the Vocabulary is limited to words of a simple and concrete meaning.

In the selection of types for Declension and Conjugation, and in the phraseology employed, Kennedy's *Shorter Latin Primer* has been closely followed, it being intended that the use of this little book should precede that of the ordinary Grammars.

It is not necessary that the whole of the preliminary matter should be mastered before beginning Exercise I; the remarks on the Sentence, Nouns, Adjectives, and Verbs are placed here for convenience of reference, and can be studied as occasion requires; the Definitions, however, and the English Verb in Latin form should be thoroughly learned at first.

The practice of reading or writing the Exercises should not interfere with the constant repetition (**vīvā vōce**) of the types so far as they have been learned. For this purpose the Accidence, which is taught progressively in the body of the book, is exhibited in a collected form at the end.

To meet the repeated demand for more advanced Exercises on the lines of the present book, a sequel has been published under the title *Second Steps in Latin*.

F. RITCHIE.

CONTENTS

FIRST STEPS IN LATIN

DEFINITIONS

A **Noun** (Substantive) is the Name of a Person or Thing; as, ' James,' ' dog,' ' book,' ' London.'

An **Adjective** is a word which describes a Person or Thing; as, *little* dog, *red* book, *many* books.

A **Verb** is a word which tells what a Person or Thing does or has done to it; as, ' sleep,' ' strike,' ' to be struck.'

(i) Verbs are *Intransitive* when the action does not pass beyond the doer; as, I *sleep*, the boy *runs*, snakes *creep*.

(ii) Verbs are *Transitive* when the action passes on to another Person or Thing. The word denoting this Person or Thing is called the Object; as, ' I strike the table.' Here ' table ' is the Object to the Verb ' strike.'

(iii) Verbs are *Copulative* when they join together two words, one of which names a thing and the other describes it; as, ' the water is deep.' Here ' is ' joins ' water ' and ' deep ' and is a Copulative Verb. The word that *describes* is called the Complement; thus, ' deep ' describes water, and is the Complement.

THE SENTENCE

Every **Sentence** has two parts, namely:—

1. The *Subject*, *i.e.* the word denoting the Person or Thing about which something is said.

2. The *Predicate*, *i.e.* the word or words denoting that which is said about it.

Examples—

SUBJECT	PREDICATE
(i) Birds	fly
(ii) We	eat bread
(iii) The man	is old

[The Subject of a Sentence may be found by asking the question Who? or What? with the Verb; thus, ' Birds fly.' Who or what fly? *Ans.* ' Birds.' The Predicate may be found by asking the question, What about the Subject? thus, ' The man is old.' What about the man? *Ans.* He is old—' is old ' is the Predicate.]

The *Subject* is always a Noun, or some word or words used as Nouns.

The *Predicate* is always a Verb, or at least contains a Verb; but as Verbs are of three kinds the Predicate has three forms. (See examples given above.)

(i) When the Verb is Intransitive, the Subject and Verb together make complete sense, and the Predicate need contain nothing but the Verb.

(ii) When the Verb is Transitive, an Object is required to complete the Sentence, and the Verb and Object together make up the Predicate.

(iii) When the Verb is Copulative, a Complement is required to complete the Sentence, and the Verb and Complement together make up the Predicate.

ANALYSIS OF SIMPLE SENTENCE

The following method of Analysis will be found useful—

The Subject is marked S.

The Predicate is marked either

        (i) V.I., *i.e.* Verb Intransitive;

or

        (ii) V.T. and O., *i.e.* Verb Transitive and Object;

or

        (iii) V.C. and C., *i.e.* Verb Copulative and Complement.

The examples given above will be analysed thus—

SUBJECT	PREDICATE	
S. (i) Birds	V.I. fly	
S. (ii) We	V.T. eat	O. bread
S. (iii) The man	V.C. is	C. old

LATIN NOUNS

Inflexion.—The form of a Latin Noun is altered by Inflexion, that is, by changing the ending of the word; thus, mēnsa, *a table*; mēnsae, *of a table*.

Case.—In this way six different forms of the same Noun are obtained; these are called the six Cases of the Noun. The names of the Cases are—

1. The *Nominative*; the subject of the Sentence is in the Nominative.

2. The *Vocative*; used in addressing Persons or Things; as, ' O queen.'

3. The *Accusative*; the Object of a Transitive Verb is in the Accusative.

4. The *Genitive*; answers the question ' belonging to whom or what ? '

5. The *Dative*; answers the question ' to or for whom or what ? '

6. The *Ablative*; answers the question ' by, with, or from what ? '

Number.—Latin Nouns have Two Numbers, Singular and Plural, and each Number has a distinct set of Six Cases.

Gender.—There are Three Genders: Masculine, Feminine, and Neuter.

Declension.—A Noun is said to be ' declined ' when its various Cases are shown in order. There are Five Declensions of Latin Nouns, that is, there are Five different sets of Inflexions. The Declensions may be distinguished by the ending of the Genitive Case Singular [1]—

Declension	1st	2nd	3rd	4th	5th
Ending of Genitive	ae	ī	is	ūs	ēī

ADJECTIVES

Adjectives are declined like Nouns as regards Number and Case; but besides this their terminations sometimes indicate the Gender of the Noun to which the Adjective belongs. Thus some Adjectives have in each Case a separate form for each of the three Genders; others have in some Cases one form for Masculine and Feminine and another for Neuter, and in some Cases only one form for all three Genders.

---

[1] The termination of the Genitive Singular is given as the distinguishing mark of the Declensions, this being the method adopted in dictionaries. The terms Stem and Character are purposely avoided. It is practically useless (and to beginners very confusing) to be told that **domino** is the Stem of **dominus**. The plan of cutting off **-rum** or **-um** from the Genitive Plural in order to find the Character and so determine the Declension, presupposes that the pupil is already able to decline the Noun.

LATIN VERBS [1]

Voice. Verbs have Two Voices, namely:

1. The Active Voice, when the person or thing denoted by the Subject does something; as, **amō,** *I love.*

2. The Passive Voice, when the person or thing denoted by the Subject has something done to it; as, **amor,** *I am loved.*

[*N.B.*—Only Transitive Verbs have a complete Passive Voice.]

Tense. Each Voice has Six Tenses—

Present, Imperfect, and Future Simple,
Perfect and Aorist, Pluperfect, and Future Perfect.

(There is only one Form in Latin for both Perfect and Aorist [2] Tenses, but in English they are distinct.)

Number. Each Tense has Two Numbers, namely—
Singular and Plural.

Person. Each Number has Three Persons, namely—
First, Second, and Third.

---

[1] On pages 8 and 9 the English Verb *To teach* is conjugated in Latin form, *i.e.* the names of the Tenses are those used in conjugating a Latin Verb. It is advisable that for practice other Verbs, and especially the Verbs *love, advise, rule, hear,* should be conjugated in the same way. The strong verb *teach* is given here in preference to the Verb *love,* because it has been found that confusion arises from the similarity in sound of the various parts of the latter: *e.g. loved* and *love.*

[2] See note on p. 14.

The Tense, Number, and Person of Latin Verbs are indicated by various Endings, which are added to the Stems.[1]

In order to form the Tenses of a Latin Verb it is necessary to know three Stems—

1. **The Present Stem—**

From this are formed the Present, Imperfect, and Future Simple, both Active and Passive.

2. **The Perfect Stem—**

From this are formed the Perfect and Aorist, Pluperfect, and Future Perfect **Active.**

3. **The Supine Stem—**

From this are formed the Perfect and Aorist, Pluperfect, and Future Perfect **Passive.**

Latin Verbs are divided into four Classes, called Conjugations, according to the last letter of the Present Stem

The **First Conjugation** has its Present Stem ending in Ā.

The **Second** ,, ,, ,, ,, Ē.

The **Third** ,, ,, ,, a Consonant or U.

The **Fourth** ,, ,, ,, ,, Ī.

---

[1] Distinction of Mood is intentionally omitted here, as beyond the scope of the book.

ENGLISH VERBS

ACTIVE VOICE

Present Tense	Perfect Tense

Sing. 1. I teach
    2. You teach
    3. He, she, or it teaches
Plur. 1. We teach
    2. You teach
    3. They teach
	Sing. 1. I have taught
	    2. You have taught
	    3. He, she, or it has taught
	Plur. 1. We have taught
	    2. You have taught
	    3. They have taught

or,	**Aorist Tense**

Sing. 1. I am teaching
    2. You are teaching
    3. He, she, or it is teaching
Plur. 1. We are teaching
    2. You are teaching
    3. They are teaching
	Sing. 1. I taught
	    2. You taught
	    3. He, she, or it taught
	Plur. 1. We taught
	    2. You taught
	    3. They taught

or,	*or,*

Sing. 1. I do teach
    2. You do teach
    3. He, she, or it does teach
Plur. 1. We do teach
    2. You do teach
    3. They do teach
	Sing. 1. I did teach
	    2. You did teach
	    3. He, she, or it did teach
	Plur. 1. We did teach
	    2. You did teach
	    3. They did teach

Imperfect Tense	**Pluperfect Tense**

Sing. 1. I was teaching
    2. You were teaching
    3. He, she, or it was teaching
Plur. 1. We were teaching
    2. You were teaching
    3. They were teaching
	Sing. 1. I had taught
	    2. You had taught
	    3. He, she, or it had taught
	Plur. 1. We had taught
	    2. You had taught
	    3. They had taught

Future Simple Tense	**Future Perfect Tense**

Sing. 1. I shall teach
    2. You will teach
    3. He, she, or it will teach
Plur. 1. We shall teach
    2. You will teach
    3. They will teach
	Sing. 1. I shall have taught
	    2. You will have taught
	    3. He will have taught
	Plur. 1. We shall have taught
	    2. You will have taught
	    3. They will have taught

PASSIVE VOICE

Present Tense	Perfect Tense
Sing. 1. I am being taught 2. You are being taught 3. He, she, or it is being taught Plur. 1. We are being taught 2. You are being taught 3. They are being taught	Sing. 1. I have been taught 2. You have been taught 3. He, she, or it has been taught Plur. 1. We have been taught 2. You have been taught 3. They have been taught
or,	**Aorist Tense**
Sing. 1. I am taught 2. You are taught 3. He, she, or it is taught Plur. 1. We are taught 2. You are taught 3. They are taught	Sing. 1. I was taught 2. You were taught 3. He, she, or it was taught Plur. 1. We were taught 2. You were taught 3. They were taught
Imperfect Tense	**Pluperfect Tense**
Sing. 1. I was being taught 2. You were being taught 3. He, she, or it was being taught Plur. 1. We were being taught 2. You were being taught 3. They were being taught	Sing. 1. I had been taught 2. You had been taught 3. He, she, or it had been taught Plur. 1. We had been taught 2. You had been taught 3. They had been taught
Future Simple Tense	**Future Perfect Tense**
Sing. 1. I shall be taught 2. You will be taught 3. He, she, or it will be taught Plur. 1. We shall be taught 2. You will be taught 3. They will be taught	Sing. 1. I shall have been taught 2. You will have been taught 3. He, she, or it will have been taught Plur. 1. We shall have been taught 2. You will have been taught 3. They will have been taught

FIRST CONJUGATION : Ā-VERBS

Verbs whose Present Stem ends in **ā** belong to the First Conjugation.

Example—**Amā-re,** *to love*   Pres. Stem, **Amā-**

ACTIVE VOICE

PRESENT TENSE

The Present Tense is formed by adding Personal Endings to the Present Stem, **amā-**.

	FORMATION	EXAMPLE	ENGLISH
Sing. 1.	Present Stem +ō [1]	**am-ō**	*I love.* Obs. 1
2.	,, ,, +s	**amā-s**	*You love*
3.	,, ,, +t	**ama-t**	*He loves*
Plur. 1.	,, ,, +mus	**amā-mus**	*We love*
2.	,, ,, +tis	**amā-tis**	*You love*
3.	,, ,, +nt	**ama-nt**	*They love*

[1] [In the First Person Singular, by adding **ō** to **amā-** we get **amā-ō,** but this is contracted to **am-ō**: hence the **a** at the end of the Stem is not seen.]

Obs. 1. Remember that the Present Tense has three forms in English—

    Amō = *I love*   or *I am loving*   or *I do love*
    Amās = *You love*   ,, *You are loving* ,, *You do love*
    Amat = *He loves*   ,, *He is loving* ,, *He does love*, etc.

Obs. 2. No separate Latin word is required for ' I,' ' you,' ' he,' etc.; thus, **amat,** *he loves.* The Personal Pronouns are not used as the Subject of a Verb except for emphasis.

VOCABULARY

Ā-Verbs conjugated like **am-ō**

Cant-ō, *I sing*	*Present Stem,*	**cantā-**
Pugn-ō, *I fight*	„	**pugnā-**
Salt-ō, *I dance*	„	**saltā-**
Voc-ō, *I call*	„	**vocā-**

Nōn= *not*

EXERCISE I

1. Canta-t.
2. Pugnā-s.
3. Saltā-mus.
4. Voca-nt.
5. Cantā-tis.
6. Pugna-t.
7. Saltā-tis.
8. Vocā-mus.
9. Canta-nt.
10. Pugnā-mus.

11. Nōn salt-ō.
12. Nōn vocā-s.
13. Cantā-s.
14. Pugnā-tis.
15. Nōn voca-t.
16. Cantā-mus.
17. Nōn pugna-nt.
18. Nōn voc-ō.
19. Nōn vocā-tis.
20. Salta-nt.

1. They sing.
2. We fight.
3. You (*pl.*) dance.
4. He calls.
5. You (*sing.*) sing.
6. I do not fight.
7. He is dancing.
8. They are calling.
9. We do not sing.
10. You (*pl.*) are fighting.

11. He does not dance.
12. I am calling.
13. You (*pl.*) are not singing.
14. They fight.
15. You (*sing.*) call.
16. He is fighting.
17. You (*sing.*) dance.
18. We do not call.
19. They dance.
20. He does not fight.

First Conjugation : Ā-Verbs—*continued*

Amā-re, *to love*   *Present Stem,* **Amā-**

ACTIVE VOICE

IMPERFECT AND FUTURE SIMPLE TENSES

Both these Tenses are formed, like the Present, by adding Personal Endings to the Present Stem, **amā-.**

IMPERFECT			
	FORMATION	EXAMPLE	ENGLISH
Sing. 1	Present Stem +**bam**	amā-**bam**	*I was loving*
2	,, ,, +**bās**	amā-**bās**	*You were loving*
3	,, ,, +**bat**	amā-**bat**	*He was loving*
Plur. 1	,, ,, +**bāmus**	amā-**bāmus**	*We were loving*
2	,, ,, +**bātis**	amā-**bātis**	*You were loving*
3	,, ,, +**bant**	amā-**bant**	*They were loving*

FUTURE SIMPLE			
Sing. 1	Present Stem +**bō**	amā-**bō**	*I shall love*
2	,, ,, +**bis**	amā-**bis**	*You will love*
3	,, ,, +**bit**	amā-**bit**	*He will love*
Plur. 1	,, ,, +**bimus**	amā-**bimus**	*We shall love*
2	,, ,, +**bitis**	amā-**bitis**	*You will love*
3	,, ,, +**bunt**	amā-**bunt**	*They will love*

VOCABULARY

Laud-ō, *I praise*   *Present Stem,* **laudā-**
Rog-ō, *I ask*   „   **rogā-**

EXERCISE II

1. Saltā-bat.
2. Vocā-mus.
3. Pugnā-bit.
4. Rogā-bis.
5. Laudā-s.
6. Cantā-bitis.
7. Vocā-bant.
8. Pugnā-bunt.
9. Vocā-bās.
10. Pugnā-tis.

11. Saltā-bam.
12. Vocā-bāmus.
13. Rogā-bitis.
14. Salta-t.
15. Vocā-s.
16. Lauda-nt.
17. Laudā-bat.
18. Pugnā-bant.
19. Canta-nt.
20. Vocā-bis.

1. We shall fight.
2. He was calling.
3. They will praise.
4. You (*sing.*) fight.
5. I shall ask.
6. They were dancing.
7. We are calling.
8. He calls.
9. They will call.
10. He does not fight.

11. They were asking.
12. You (*sing.*) will praise.
13. He was not calling.
14. He is praising.
15. You (*sing.*) were fighting.
16. We do not dance.
17. You (*pl.*) were calling.
18. We were praising.
19. You (*pl.*) will sing.
20. He is dancing.

First Conjugation : Ā-Verbs—*continued*

Amare, *to love*

ACTIVE VOICE

THE PERFECT AND AORIST TENSE

This Tense is formed by adding the Personal Endings to the Perfect Stem, **amāv-**.

The Perfect Stem of any regular Verb of the First Conjugation is found by adding **v** to the Present Stem; thus—

Present Stem, **amā-** *Perfect Stem,* **amāv-**
  „   **pugnā-**   „   **pugnāv-**

	FORMATION	EXAMPLE	ENGLISH	
	Perf. Stem		Perfect	Aorist [1]
Sing. 1	+**i**	**amāv-ī**	*I have loved*	*I loved*
2	+**istī**	**amāv-istī**	*You have loved*	*You loved*
3	+**it**	**amāv-it**	*He has loved*	*He loved*
Plur. 1	+**imus**	**amāv-imus**	*We have loved*	*We loved*
2	+**istis**	**amāv-istis**	*You have loved*	*You loved*
3	+**ērunt** *or* +**ēre**	**amāv-ērunt** *or* **amāv-ēre**	*They have loved*	*They loved*

Remember there is only one form in Latin for both Perfect and Aorist; thus, **amāvī** means both *I have loved* and *I loved* or *did love*.

---

[1] The True Perfect *with* ' have ' : **amāvī** (=*I have loved*).
The Historic Perfect *without* ' have ' : **amāvī** (=*I loved* or *I did love*).

EXERCISE III

1. Rogāv-it.
2. Saltā-bat.
3. Pugnāv-imus.
4. Nōn roga-nt.
5. Vocā-bit.
6. Salta-t.
7. Laudāv-ērunt.
8. Vocāv-istī.
9. Pugnā-bimus.
10. Laudāv-it.
11. Vocā-bat.
12. Saltā-bit.
13. Nōn laudā-mus.
14. Saltāv-istis.
15. Cantāv-ērunt.
16. Nōn laudāv-ī.
17. Voca-t.
18. Vocāv-it.
19. Nōn salta-t.
20. Cantāv-istī.
21. Rogā-bātis.
22. Laudāv-imus.
23. Saltā-bitis.
24. Pugnāv-istis.

1. We have praised.
2. They danced.
3. He did not fight.
4. You (*sing.*) were calling.
5. He sings.
6. He will dance.
7. They have asked.
8. We did not praise.
9. You (*pl.*) will ask.
10. They fought.
11. They did not dance.
12. We were calling.
13. They do not praise.
14. You (*sing.*) have called.
15. We are dancing.
16. I was calling.
17. They are dancing.
18. We shall ask.
19. He has praised.
20. You (*pl.*) have asked.
21. You (*pl.*) will call.
22. We have fought.
23. You (*sing.*) are calling.
24. I did not praise.

First Conjugation : Ā-Verbs—*continued*

ACTIVE VOICE

THE PLUPERFECT AND THE FUTURE PERFECT TENSES

Both these Tenses are formed, like the Perfect and Aorist, by adding Personal Endings to the Perfect Stem, **amāv-.**

PLUPERFECT			
	FORMATION	EXAMPLE	ENGLISH
Sing. 1	Pf. Stem +**eram**	amāv-**eram**	*I had loved*
2	,, +**erās**	amāv-**erās**	*You had loved*
3	,, +**erat**	amāv-**erat**	*He had loved*
Plur. 1	,, +**erāmus**	amāv-**erāmus**	*We had loved*
2	,, +**erātis**	amāv-**erātis**	*You had loved*
3	,, +**erant**	amāv-**erant**	*They had loved*
FUTURE PERFECT			
Sing. 1	Pf. Stem +**erō**	amāv-**erō**	*I shall have loved*
2	,, +**eris**	amāv-**eris**	*You will have loved*
3	,, +**erit**	amāv-**erit**	*He will have loved*
Plur. 1	,, +**erimus**	amāv-**erimus**	*We shall have loved*
2	,, +**eritis**	amāv-**eritis**	*You will have loved*
3	,, +**erint**	amāv-**erint**	*They will have loved*

In the sentence **amat**=*he loves*, the Personal Pronoun (he) is omitted in Latin unless it is emphatic, but the Subject may also be a separate word; thus, **Puella amat,** *the girl loves.*

RULE.—**The Verb must agree in Person with its Subject**; thus, **puella,** the Subject, is of the Third Person, therefore the Verb **amat** is also of the Third Person.

VOCABULARY

Vol-ō, *I fly* Present Stem, volā- Hasta, *a spear*
Vulner-ō, *I wound* „ vulnerā- Puella, *a girl*
Rēgīna, *a queen*

EXERCISE IV

1. Vocāv-erat.
2. Pugnāv-erit.
3. Hasta volā-bat.
4. Pugnā-bit.
5. Vocāv-erimus.
6. Vulnerā-mus.
7. Rogāv-eris.
8. Saltāv-erās.
9. Puella lauda-t.
10. Vocāv-ērunt.
11. Nōn saltā-bimus.
12. Rogāv-erātis.
13. Puella saltāv-erat.
14. Vulnerāv-ērunt.
15. Vulnerā-bunt.
16. Laudāv-erit.
17. Vulnerā-tis.
18. Cantāv-erant.
19. Vocāv-erint.
20. Pugnāv-ērunt.

1. They had called.
2. He will have asked.
3. We have fought.
4. You (*pl.*) were dancing.
5. The girl will praise.
6. We sang.
7. They will have sung.
8. You (*pl.*) did not praise.
9. The spear flies.
10. We had wounded.
11. They did not fight.
12. You (*sing.*) had praised.
13. The queen will ask.
14. We shall have fought.
15. He had sung.
16. The spear will wound.
17. They do not fight.
18. We were calling.
19. The girl had danced.
20. You (*sing.*) will have fought.

NOUNS

FIRST DECLENSION

Nouns whose Genitive Singular ends in **ae** belong to the First Declension. The Nominative ends in **a**.

The Cases are formed as follows:—

	SINGULAR		PLURAL	
Nom.	Mēns-a	a table (f.)	Mēns-ae	tables
Voc.	Mēns-a	O table	Mēns-ae	O tables
Acc.	Mēns-am	a table	Mēns-ās	tables
Gen.	Mēns-ae	of a table	Mēns-ārum	of tables
Dat.	Mēns-ae	to or for a table	Mēns-īs	to or for tables
Abl.	Mēns-ā	by, with, or from a table	Mēns-īs	by, with, or from tables

Most Nouns of the First Declension are of the Feminine Gender.

RULE.—**The Subject of the Sentence is in the Nominative Case, and the Verb must agree in Number with its Subject.**

That is, if the Subject is Singular, the Verb must be Singular.

          „   „   Plural,   „   „   Plural.

Thus, in the sentence *The girls love*, the Subject, ' *girls*,' is Plural, therefore the Verb must also be plural, and the Latin will be ' **Puellae amant.**'

Remember that the Verb must also agree with its Subject in Person.

VOCABULARY

Decline—

Epistul-a, -ae, f., *a letter*   **Sagitt-a, -ae,** f., *an arrow*

EXERCISE V

Point out the Subject and Predicate in each Sentence.

1. Hastae vulnera-nt.
2. Rēgīna laudā-bat.
3. Nōn pugnāv-erāmus.
4. Puellae saltā-bunt.
5. Vocāv-ērunt.
6. Rēgīna cantāv-erit.
7. Puellae vocā-bant.
8. Nōn amā-tis.
9. Rēgīnae laudāv-erant.
10. Sagittae vulnerāv-ērunt.
11. Epistula laudā-bit.
12. Cantāv-erāmus.
13. Laudāv-istis.
14. Nōn pugnā-bātis.
15. Rēgīnae salta-nt.
16. Puella vocāv-erit.
17. Puellae vocāv-erant.
18. Hastae vulnerā-bunt.
19. Nōn saltāv-istī.
20. Vocāv-erint.

1. The girls do not call.
2. The queen will fight.
3. The spears wounded.
4. You (*pl.*) did not dance.
5. I had not fought.
6. The queens praised.
7. The girls were dancing.
8. The spears will fly.
9. We had sung.
10. You (*sing.*) fought.
11. The arrows were flying.
12. The queen had praised.
13. We shall have sung.
14. You (*pl.*) were asking.
15. The queen does not dance.
16. They had fought.
17. We do not praise.
18. The girl has not sung.
19. They have asked.
20. We are not praising.

SECOND CONJUGATION: Ē-VERBS

Verbs whose Present Stem ends in **ē** belong to the Second Conjugation.

Example—**Monē-re,** *to advise*

Present Stem, **monē-**   *Perfect Stem,* **monu-**

ACTIVE VOICE

TENSES FORMED FROM THE PRESENT STEM **Monē-**

[The Personal Endings are the same as in the First Conjugation]

PRESENT			
	FORMATION	EXAMPLE	ENGLISH
Sing. 1	Pres. Stem +**ō**	**mone-ō**	*I advise,* p. 10, *Obs.* 1
2	,, ,, +**s**	**monē-s**	*You advise*
3	,, ,, +**t**	**mone-t**	*He advises*
Plur. 1	,, ,, +**mus**	**monē-mus**	*We advise*
2	,, ,, +**tis**	**monē-tis**	*You advise*
3	,, ,, +**nt**	**mone-nt**	*They advise*
IMPERFECT			
Sing. 1	Pres. Stem +**bam**	**monē-bam**	*I was advising*
2	,, ,, +**bās**	**monē-bās**	*You were advising*
3	,, ,, +**bat**	**monē-bat**	*He was advising*
Plur. 1	,, ,, +**bāmus**	**monē-bāmus**	*We were advising*
2	,, ,, +**bātis**	**monē-bātis**	*You were advising*
3	,, ,, +**bant**	**monē-bant**	*They were advising*
FUTURE SIMPLE			
Sing. 1	Pres. Stem +**bō**	**monē-bō**	*I shall advise*
2	,, ,, +**bis**	**monē-bis**	*You will advise*
3	,, ,, +**bit**	**monē-bit**	*He will advise*
Plur. 1	,, ,, +**bimus**	**monē-bimus**	*We shall advise*
2	,, ,, +**bitis**	**monē-bitis**	*You will advise*
3	,, ,, +**bunt**	**monē-bunt**	*They will advise*

RULE.—**The Object of a Transitive Verb is in the Accusative Case.**

Thus—

	Subject	*Object*	*Transitive Verb*
	The queen	the girl	loves
	Rēgīna (Nom.)	**puellam** (Accus.)	**amat**

VOCABULARY

Verbs of Second Conjugation like **mone-ō**

Doce-ō, *I teach*	*Present Stem*, **docē-**
Tene-ō, *I hold*	„ **tenē-**
Time-ō, *I fear*	„ **timē-**

EXERCISE VI

[*N.B.*—In Latin the Object is generally placed before its Verb]

Point out the Subject and Object (where there is one).

1. Puellam docē-mus.
2. Hastās tenē-bant.
3. Hastam tene-t.
4. Rēgīnam timē-bunt.
5. Puellae nōn time-nt.
6. Rēgīna saltāv-erat.
7. Epistulam tenē-bam.
8. Hastae vulnera-nt.
9. Hastās nōn timē-bo.
10. Puellās docē-tis.
11. Nōn pugnāv-istī.
12. Rēgīnam voca-t.
13. Hasta volāv-erit.
14. Puellam laudā-mus.
15. Hastās tenē-batis.
16. Nōn docē-bitis.
17. Epistulam tene-t.
18. Hastam timē-bat.
19. Rēgīnae time-nt.
20. Nōn pugnāv-erāmus.

1. We fear the queen.
2. You (*pl.*) teach the girls.
3. The girl will fear.
4. They hold a spear.
5. You (*pl.*) were not teaching.
6. You (*sing.*) fear.
7. We had not danced.
8. He praised the letter.
9. I shall teach the girl.
10. He is not fighting.
11. They were holding letters.
12. You (*pl.*) will fear the spear.
13. You (*sing.*) did not call.
14. Spears had wounded.
15. They will teach girls.
16. The girls were fearing.
17. You (*pl.*) will have fought.
18. You (*sing.*) teach the queen.
19. They fear the spears.
20. He called the girl.

Second Conjugation : Ē-Verbs—*continued*
Monē-re, *to advise*
Present Stem, **monē-**   *Perfect Stem,* **monu-**

ACTIVE VOICE
TENSES FORMED FROM THE PERFECT STEM **Monu-**

The Perfect Stem of any regular Verb of the Second Conjugation is found by changing the last letter of the Present Stem from **ē** into **u**.

[The Personal Endings are the same as in the First Conjugation]

		FORMATION	EXAMPLE	ENGLISH	
PERFECT AND AORIST					
				Perfect	Aorist
		Perf. Stem			
Sing.	1	+ī	monu-ī	I have ⎫	I advised
	2	+istī	monu-istī	You have ⎬	You advised
	3	+it	monu-it	He has	He advised
Plur.	1	+imus	monu-imus	We have ⎬ *advised*	We advised
	2	+istis	monu-istis	You have	You advised
	3	+ērunt	monu-ērunt	They have ⎭	They advised
		or +ēre	*or* monu-ēre		
PLUPERFECT					
		Perf. Stem			
Sing.	1	+eram	monu-eram	I had advised	
	2	+erās	monu-erās	You had advised	
	3	+erat	monu-erat	He had advised	
Plur.	1	+erāmus	monu-erāmus	We had advised	
	2	+erātis	monu-erātis	You had advised	
	3	+erant	monu-erant	They had advised	
FUTURE PERFECT					
		Perf. Stem			
Sing.	1	+erō	monu-erō	I shall have advised	
	2	+eris	monu-eris	You will have advised	
	3	+erit	monu-erit	He will have advised	
Plur.	1	+erimus	monu-erimus	We shall have advised	
	2	+eritis	monu-eritis	You will have advised	
	3	+erint	monu-erint	They will have advised	

Obs. Distinguish carefully between the ' have ' in *I have a letter*, **Epistulam habeō**, and that in *I have advised*, **monu-ī**.

VOCABULARY

Aqu-a, ae, f., *water* Īr-a, -ae, f., *anger*
Habeō, *I have* Present Stem, habē-

EXERCISE VII

Point out the Subject and Object.

1. Hastam tenu-ī.
2. Puellās docu-erās.
3. Rēgīna timu-erit.
4. Sagittās tenu-imus.
5. Aquam timu-erātis.
6. Epistulās habē-tis.
7. Puellae saltāv-ērunt.
8. Rēgīna hastam habē-bit.
9. Puellam laudāv-erant.
10. Puellae timu-ērunt.
11. Sagittam nōn habu-it.
12. Puellam docu-istī.
13. Rēgīna monu-erit.
14. Sagittae volā-bunt.
15. Sagittās tenē-tis.
16. Nōn monu-istis.
17. Hastās habu-erant.
18. Rēgīnam docu-eris.
19. Puellae cantā-bant.
20. Rēgīnam timu-erit.

1. We held spears.
2. You (*pl.*) do not fear anger.
3. The girl had not taught.
4. You (*sing.*) taught the girl.
5. We have had the letter.
6. I did not fear the arrow.
7. We do not praise the girl.
8. We shall not have water.
9. He was teaching the girl.
10. They had held the arrows.
11. The queen will have advised.
12. You (*pl.*) are not praising.
13. They fear the water.
14. The girls had not fought.
15. I did not praise the girl.
16. The queen has not had the letters.
17. The arrow has wounded.
18. The spears did not wound.
19. You (*sing.*) had taught the queen.
20. You (*pl.*) have the letter.

NOUNS

SECOND DECLENSION

Nouns whose Genitive Singular ends in **i** belong to the Second Declension.

The Nominative ends in **us or er,** if the Noun is Masculine or Feminine.

The Nominative ends in **um,** if the Noun is Neuter.

MASCULINE

SINGULAR			PLURAL	
Nom.	**Domin-us**	*a lord (m.)*	**Domin-i**	*lords*
Voc.	**Domin-e**	*O lord*	**Domin-i**	*O lords*
Acc.	**Domin-um**	*a lord*	**Domin-ōs**	*lords*
Gen.	**Domin-ī**	*of a lord*	**Domin-ōrum**	*of lords*
Dat.	**Domin-ō**	*to or for a lord*	**Domin-īs**	*to or for lords*
Abl.	**Domin-ō**	*by, with, or from a lord* [1]	**Domin-īs**	*by, with, or from lords* [1]
Nom.	**Magister**	*a master (m.)*	**Magistr-ī**	*masters*
Voc.	**Magister**	*O master*	**Magistr-ī**	*O masters*
Acc.	**Magistr-um**	*a master*	**Magistr-ōs**	*masters*
Gen.	**Magistr-ī**	*of a master*	**Magistr-ōrum**	*of masters*
Dat.	**Magistr-ō**	*to or for a master*	**Magistr-īs**	*to or for masters*
Abl.	**Magistr-ō**	*by, with, or from a master* [1]	**Magistr-īs**	*by, with, or from masters* [1]

The Case-endings of **dominus** and **magister** are exactly alike except in the Nominative and Vocative Singular.

Observe that in declining **magister** the **e** is dropped in all Cases except Nominative and Vocative Singular.

---

[1] A Latin Preposition is required to give this meaning to the Ablative of **dominus** and **magister,** or of any word which is the name of a person.

VOCABULARY

Like **Dominus**	Like **Magister**
Serv-us, -ī, m., *a slave*	Liber, librī, m., *a book*
Amīc-us, -ī, m., *a friend*	

EXERCISE VIII

Point out the Subject and Object.

1. Magister servum lauda-t.
2. Puellae librōs tenē-bant.
3. Rēgīna amīcum habe-t.
4. Dominum nōn timu-ērunt.
5. Amīcī servōs vocā-bunt.
6. Servī nōn pugnāv-erant.
7. Rēgīna hastam tenu-erit.
8. Amīcōs laudā-bāmus.
9. Sagittae volāv-ērunt.
10. Puellās docu-erimus.
11. Servī dominum time-nt.
12. Rēgīna librum lauda-t.
13. Hasta servum vulnerā-bit.
14. Puella aquam timu-it.
15. Hastās nōn habē-bimus.
16. Magister puellās doce-t.
17. Magistrōs amā-bātis.
18. Servī sagittās tenē-bunt.
19. Rēgīnam vulnerāv-istī.
20. Librōs nōn laudāv-istis.

1. The slaves feared the queen.
2. The friend will hold spears.
3. The girl fears the slaves.
4. I did not praise the girl.
5. The master had taught.
6. We shall praise the book.
7. You (*s.*) do not fear water.
8. I shall have a slave.
9. The girls love the queen.
10. They will not have fought.
11. The spear wounded the girl.
12. You (*s.*) were holding a book.
13. The girls have not sung.
14. You (*pl.*) called the slaves.
15. The queen loves the friends.
16. We fear the master.
17. You (*pl.*) had held the spears.
18. We did not call the girl.
19. We were asking the slaves.
20. They have the letters.

Second Declension—*continued*

MASCULINE

A few words ending in **er** do not drop the **e** in declension as **magister** does.

	SINGULAR		PLURAL	
Nom.	**Puer**	*a boy (m.)*	**Puer-ī**	*boys*
Voc.	**Puer**	*O boy*	**Puer-ī**	*O boys*
Acc.	**Puer-um**	*a boy*	**Puer-ōs**	*boys*
Gen.	**Puer-ī**	*of a boy*	**Puer-ōrum**	*of boys*
Dat.	**Puer-ō**	*to or for a boy*	**Puer-īs**	*to or for boys*
Abl.	**Puer-ō**	*by, with, or from a boy*[1]	**Puer-īs**	*by, with, or from boys*[1]

NEUTER

The Nominative Singular of Neuter Nouns of the Second Declension ends in **um**.

	SINGULAR		PLURAL	
Nom.	**Bell-um**	*war (n.)*	**Bell-a**	*wars*
Voc.	**Bell-um**	*O war*	**Bell-a**	*O wars*
Acc.	**Bell-um**	*war*	**Bell-a**	*wars*
Gen.	**Bell-ī**	*of war*	**Bell-ōrum**	*of wars*
Dat.	**Bell-ō**	*to or for war*	**Bell-īs**	*to or for wars*
Abl.	**Bell-ō**	*by, with, or from war*	**Bell-īs**	*by, with, or from wars*

In all the Declensions the Nominative, Vocative, and Accusative of Neuter Nouns are alike, and the Nominative, Vocative, and Accusative Plural end in **a**.

---

[1] A Preposition is required. See p. 24.

VOCABULARY

Dōnum, -ī, n., *a gift*   **Tēl-um, -ī,** n., *a dart*
Terre-ō, *I frighten.*   *Present Stem,* **terrē-**

EXERCISE IX

1. Tēla puerum terre-nt.
2. Puer dōna lauda-t.
3. Puerōs vocā-bās.
4. Tēla tenē-bimus.
5. Puella librum habe-t.
6. Amicōs laudāv-istis.
7. Hasta servum vulnera-t.
8. Rēgīna nōn saltāv-erit.
9. Puellae aquam time-nt.
10. Servī puerum amā-bant.
11. Puerī tēla tenē-bunt.
12. Hastās nōn habu-imus.
13. Rēgīnae vocāv-erant.
14. Rēgīnam amāv-imus.
15. Puer scrvōs rogā-bat.
16. Magister puerōs docu-it.
17. Sagittae vulnerā-bunt.
18. Dominus servum lauda-t.
19. Epistulās tenu-erātis.
20. Puellae saltāv-ērunt.

1. The boys loved books.
2. We did not fear war.
3. The queen was calling.
4. You (*pl.*) have taught boys.
5. I shall praise the gifts.
6. The slaves feared water.
7. Boys will hold arrows.
8. The darts wound the boys.
9. The girls are not dancing.
10. We do not have slaves.
11. You (*s.*) will have sung.
12. The girl held letters.
13. Masters will teach boys.
14. Slaves fear darts.
15. We had asked the girl.
16. They praised the gifts.
17. The queen will not fight.
18. You (*pl.*) were not singing.
19. They frightened the girl.
20. The slaves had fought.

THIRD CONJUGATION : CONSONANT VERBS

Verbs whose Present Stem ends in a Consonant [1] belong to the Third Conjugation.

Example—**Reg-ere,** *to rule*
Present Stem, **reg-** *Perfect Stem,* **rēx-**

ACTIVE VOICE
TENSES FORMED FROM THE PRESENT STEM **Reg-**

		FORMATION		EXAMPLE	ENGLISH
PRESENT					
Sing.	1	Present Stem	+ō	reg-ō	*I rule*
	2	,, ,,	+is	reg-is	*You rule*
	3	,, ,,	+it	reg-it	*He rules*
Plur.	1	,, ,,	+imus	reg-imus	*We rule*
	2	,, ,,	+itis	reg-itis	*You rule*
	3	,, ,,	+unt	reg-unt	*They rule*
IMPERFECT					
Sing.	1	Present Stem	+ēbam	reg-ēbam	*I was ruling*
	2	,, ,,	+ēbās	reg-ēbās	*You were ruling*
	3	,, ,,	+ēbat	reg-ēbat	*He was ruling*
Plur.	1	,, ,,	+ēbāmus	reg-ēbāmus	*We were ruling*
	2	,, ,,	+ēbātis	reg-ēbātis	*You were ruling*
	3	,, ,,	+ēbant	reg-ēbant	*They were ruling*
FUTURE SIMPLE					
Sing.	1	Present Stem	+am	reg-am	*I shall rule*
	2	,, ,,	+ēs	reg-ēs	*You will rule*
	3	,, ,,	+et	reg-et	*He will rule*
Plur.	1	,, ,,	+ēmus	reg-ēmus	*We shall rule*
	2	,, ,,	+ētis	reg-ētis	*You will rule*
	3	,, ,,	+ent	reg-ent	*They will rule*

The Engl.-Lat. sentences of the following Exercises may be analysed according to the method described on page 3. When the Subject is not given, but we know from the ending whether it is of the First, Second, or Third Person and whether it is Singular or Plural, S. should be placed over the termination, thus—

V.I.   S.   S.   V.I.
Saltā-mus = *We dance*

---

[1] Or **u.**

VOCABULARY

Verbs of Third Conjugation

Dūc-ō, *I lead*	*Present Stem,* **dūc-**	*Perfect Stem,* **dūx-**	
Mitt-ō, *I send*	„ **mitt-**	„ **mīs-**	
Scrīb-ō, *I write*	„ **scrīb-**	„ **scrīps-**	

EXERCISE X

S. O.

1. Puer librum scrīb-ēbat.
2. Servōs mitt-ent.
3. Puer aquam time-t.
4. Puerum nōn mitt-unt.
5. Librōs scrīb-ēbat.
6. Epistulam scrīb-ētis.
7. Puerōs docu-ērunt.
8. Puer dōna mitt-et.
9. Puella librum scrīb-it.
10. Servum nōn mitt-itis.

O. V.T. S.

11. Puellās dūc-ēbat.
12. Servus puerum dūc-et.
13. Amīcī dōna mitt-unt.
14. Librōs habu-erāmus.
15. Puellās dūc-itis.
16. Magistrum vulnerāv-istī.
17. Rēgīnās docu-erāmus.
18. Sagittas timu-ērunt.
19. Servī tēla mitt-ent.
20. Puerī servōs voca-nt.

Analyse the following Sentences :—

1. We shall send a slave.
2. The queen writes books.
3. You (*s.*) were leading a boy.
4. Friends will send gifts.
5. We write letters.
6. The boys were writing.
7. The girls loved books.
8. We had taught boys.
9. You (*pl.*) send arrows.
10. They had called a slave.
11. The girls will dance.
12. The queen had a spear.
13. They will send letters.
14. We are leading boys.
15. We shall write books.
16. The master taught girls.
17. We shall praise the queen.
18. You (*pl.*) had held letters.
19. The girl will send gifts.
20. Friends write letters.

Third Conjugation : Consonant Verbs—*continued*
Reg-ere, *to rule*
Present Stem, **reg-** *Perfect Stem,* **rēx-**

ACTIVE VOICE
TENSES FORMED FROM THE PERFECT STEM Rēx-

The Perf. Stem of Verbs of the Third Conjugation cannot be found from the Pres. Stem; it must be looked out.

[The Personal Endings are the same as in First and Second Conjugations]

	FORMATION	EXAMPLE	Perfect	Aorist
PERFECT AND AORIST				
	Perf. Stem			
Sing. 1	+ī	rēx-ī	*I have ruled*	*I ruled*
2	+istī	rēx-istī	*You have ruled*	*You ruled*
3	+it	rēx-it	*He has ruled*	*He ruled*
Plur. 1	+imus	rēx-imus	*We have ruled*	*We ruled*
2	+istis	rēx-istis	*You have ruled*	*You ruled*
3	+ērunt	rēx-ērunt	*They have ruled*	*They ruled*
	or +ēre	*or* rēx-ēre		

PLUPERFECT			
	Perf. Stem		
Sing. 1	+eram	rēx-eram	*I had ruled*
2	+erās	rēx-erās	*You had ruled*
3	+erat	rēx-erat	*He had ruled*
Plur. 1	+erāmus	rēx-erāmus	*We had ruled*
2	+erātis	rēx-erātis	*You had ruled*
3	+erant	rēx-erant	*They had ruled*

FUTURE PERFECT			
	Perf. Stem		
Sing. 1	+erō	rēx-erō	*I shall have ruled*
2	+eris	rēx-eris	*You will have ruled*
3	+erit	rēx-erit	*He will have ruled*
Plur. 1	+erimus	rēx-erimus	*We shall have ruled*
2	+eritis	rēx-eritis	*You will have ruled*
3	+erint	rēx-erint	*They will have ruled*

RULE.—When the Subject consists of two or more Nouns joined by ' and,' the Verb must be Plural; thus, **Puer et puella canta-nt,** *the boy and the girl sing.* When the Object consists of two or more Nouns, joined by ' and,' both must be in the Accus.; thus, **Puerum et puellam amō,** *I love the boy and the girl.*

VOCABULARY

Fili-ūs, -ī, m., *a son*   **Perīcul-um, -ī,** n., *a danger*
Nūnti-us, -ī, m., *a messenger*   **Iūlia, -ae,** f., *Julia*
Vīt-ō, *I avoid,*   **Present Stem, vītā-**
Et, *and*

EXERCISE XI

s.   o.   v.t.

1. Rēgīna nūntiōs nōn mīs-erat.
2. Puerī epistulās scrīps-ērunt.
3. Servus puerum et puellam dūx-erit.
4. Puer et puella dōnum mīs-erant.
5. Librōs et epistulās scrīps-erāmus.
6. Magister fīlium et puellam docu-it.
7. Rēgīna et Iūlia dōna mitt-ent.
8. Puellae perīcula nōn vītāv-erant.
9. Puer et servus aquam time-nt.
10. Tēla et sagittam timu-istis.
11. Servōs et nūntiōs vocāv-erātis.
12. Perīculum Iūliam nōn terrē-bit.

1. The boys and the girls wrote letters.
2. We had sent a slave and a messenger.
3. The queen will have sent arrows and spears.
4. The slaves had led the boy and the girl.
5. We have written letters and books.
6. The son will send messengers.
7. The girl and the boy were calling the queen.
8. The spears wounded the queen and the slave.
9. You had sent books and gifts.
10. Julia and the girls will avoid the danger.
11. The boys have darts and arrows.
12. The dangers frighten the master and the queen.

ADJECTIVES

Adjectives are words which qualify Nouns, and as Nouns are of various Genders, Adjectives are declined in different forms according to the Gender.

Adjectives of Three Terminations are those which have one form for the Masculine Gender, another for the Feminine, and a third for the Neuter. Thus—

The Masculine is declined like a Masculine Noun of the Second Declension.

The Feminine is declined like a Noun of First Declension.

The Neuter is declined like a Neuter Noun of Second Declension.

Bonus = *good*

	SINGULAR			PLURAL		
	Masc.	Fem.	Neut.	Masc.	Fem.	Neut.
Nom.	Bon-us	bon-a	bon-um	Bon-ī	bon-ae	bon-a
Voc.	Bon-e	bon-a	bon-um	Bon-ī	bon-ae	bon-a
Acc.	Bon-um	bon-am	bon-um	Bon-ōs	bon-ās	bon-a
Gen.	Bon-ī	bon-ae	bon-ī	Bon-ōrum	bon-ārum	bon-ōrum
Dat.	Bon-ō	bon-ae	bon-ō	Bon-īs	bon-īs	bon-īs
Abl.	Bon-ō	bon-ā	bon-ō	Bon-īs	bon-īs	bon-īs

Bonus is declined in the Masculine like **dominus**, in the Feminine like **mēnsa**, and in the Neuter like **bellum**.

RULE.—An Adjective must be of the same Gender, Case, and Number as the Noun which it qualifies; thus, **Rēgina bona**, *a good queen*. **Rēgina** is Nominative Singular Feminine, therefore **bona** must also be Nominative Singular Feminine to agree with **rēgina**.

VOCABULARY

Magn-us, -a, -um, *great*	**Me-us, -a, -um,** *my, mine*
Long-us, -a, -um, *long*	**Tu-us, -a, -um,** *your, yours*
Parv-us, -a, -um, *small, little*	**Mult-us, -a, -um,** *many*

EXERCISE XII

[*N.B.*—In Latin the Adjective generally stands after the Noun which it qualifies. But Adjectives signifying number or quantity, such as **multus,** stand before their nouns.]

1. Servī meī scrīb-ent.
2. Hastam longam time-t.
3. Rēgīna bona voca-t.
4. Puer parvus scrīps-erat.
5. Hastās longās habe-ō.
6. Fīlium meum mīs-it.
7. Librōs longōs scrīb-is.
8. Perīculum magnum vīta-t.
9. Librum parvum tenē-tis.
10. Multa dōna mitt-ēs.
11. Sagittās tuās timē-mus.
12. Servum tuum vocāv-istī.
13. Fīlius tuus servum meum docē-bat.
14. Rēgīna magna librōs tuōs laudāv-it.
15. Nūntius epistulās meās tenu-it.
16. Dōna magna et multās epistulās mīs-imus.
17. Amīcī tuī fīlium meum docu-erant.
18. Multōs librōs et epistulās longās scrīps-istī.

1. Your son has written a long letter.
2. My slaves had led the little girls.
3. We shall have sent great books.
4. You were holding arrows and long spears.
5. The queen praised my gifts and your letters.
6. The dangers do not frighten the little girl.
7. We have sent many slaves and messengers.
8. The good queen will praise the little boys.
9. The long spear has not wounded my slave.
10. Your books will teach the boys and girls.
11. The master was teaching many boys.
12. We have written a great book and many letters.

Adjectives—*continued*

Besides Adjectives in **-us, -a, -um,** there are others of Three Terminations in **-er, -a, -um.**

Niger = *black*

	SINGULAR			PLURAL		
	Masc.	Fem.	Neut.	Masc.	Fem.	Neut.
Nom. & Voc.	Niger	nigr-a	nigr-um	Nigr-ī	nigr-ae	nigr-a
Acc.	Nigr-um	nigr-am	nigr-um	Nigr-ōs	nigr-ās	nigr-a
Gen.	Nigr-ī	nigr-ae	nigr-ī	Nigr-ōrum	nigr-ārum	nigr-ōrum
Dat.	Nigr-ō	nigr-ae	nigr-ō	Nigr-īs	nigr-īs	nigr-īs
Abl.	Nigr-ō	nigr-ā	nigr-ō	Nigr-īs	nigr-īs	nigr-īs

Tener = *tender*

	SINGULAR			PLURAL		
	Masc.	Fem.	Neut.	Masc.	Fem.	Neut.
Nom. & Voc.	Tener	tener-a	tener-um	Tener-ī	tener-ae	tener-a
Acc.	Tener-um	tener-am	tener-um	Tener-ōs	tener-ās	tener-a
Gen.	Tener-ī	tener-ae	tener-ī	Tener-ōrum	tener-ārum	tener-ōrum
Dat.	Tener-ō	tener-ae	tener-ō	Tener-īs	tener-īs	tener-īs
Abl.	Tener-ō	tener-ā	tener-ō	Tener-is	tener-īs	tener-īs

Niger is declined in the Masculine like **magister,** and drops the **e.**
Tener „ „ „ **puer,** and keeps the **e.**
Both are declined in the Feminine like **mēnsa,** and in the Neuter like **bellum.**

N.B.—**Tuus** = *your,* when speaking to one person.
Vester = *your,* „ „ to more than one person.
Always use ' **tuus** ' for *your,* unless it is clear that more than one person is being addressed.

VOCABULARY

Like **Niger**	Like **Tener**
Pul-cher, -chra, -chrum, *beautiful*	**Miser, -a, -um,** *wretched*
Nos-ter, -tra, -trum, *our, ours*	
Ves-ter, -tra, -trum, *your, yours*	

EXERCISE XIII

s.   o.   v.t.

1. Puerī parvī servōs nigrōs timē-bunt.
2. Servī nostrī multās hastās tenu-ērunt.
3. Rēgīna nostra puerōs bonōs laudā-bit.
4. Puellae pulchrae amīcum vestrum dūx-ērunt.
5. Puerōs parvōs et puellās tenerās nōn timē-mus.
6. Fīlium meum et servōs vestrōs docu-ī.
7. Multa tēla et hastās longās habu-istī.
8. Puella pulchra servum miserum dūc-ēbat.
9. Fīliī nostrī dōna tua laudā-bunt.
10. Amīcī vestrī perīculum magnum vītā-bunt.
11. Dōna magna et multōs librōs mīs-erātis.
12. Puerī parvī epistulās parvās scrīb-unt.

1. Our sons were calling your slaves.
2. The black slaves feared the long spears.
3. We praised the beautiful girl and the little boy.
4. You (*sing.*) will teach your son and our slaves.
5. The good queen had avoided many dangers.
6. Our friends write many books and long letters.
7. We shall have praised our friends.
8. Our spears wounded the wretched queen.
9. You (*pl.*) will have sent your friends.
10. The little boys will have the beautiful gifts.
11. You (*sing.*) had sent your son and my friend.
12. The tender boys and the slaves did not fight.

FOURTH CONJUGATION: I-VERBS

Verbs whose Present Stem ends in **i** belong to the Fourth Conjugation.

Example—**Audī-re,** *to hear*

Present Stem, **audī-**   *Perfect Stem,* **audīv-**

ACTIVE VOICE

TENSES FORMED FROM THE PRESENT STEM **Audī-**

	FORMATION		EXAMPLE	ENGLISH
PRESENT				
Sing. 1	Pres. Stem	+**ō**	**audi-ō**	*I hear*
2	,, ,,	+**s**	**audi-s**	*You hear*
3	,, ,,	+**t**	**audi-t**	*He hears*
Plur. 1	,, ,,	+**mus**	**audī-mus**	*We hear*
2	,, ,,	+**tis**	**audī-tis**	*You hear*
3	,, ,,	+**unt**	**audi-unt**	*They hear*
IMPERFECT				
Sing. 1	Pres. Stem	+**ēbam**	**audi-ēbam**	*I was hearing*
2	,, ,,	+**ēbās**	**audi-ēbās**	*You were hearing*
3	,, ,,	+**ēbat**	**audi-ēbat**	*He was hearing*
Plur. 1	,, ,,	+**ēbāmus**	**audi-ēbāmus**	*We were hearing*
2	,, ,,	+**ēbātis**	**audi-ēbātis**	*You were hearing*
3	,, ,,	+**ēbant**	**audi-ēbant**	*They were hearing*
FUTURE SIMPLE				
Sing. 1	Pres. Stem	+**am**	**audi-am**	*I shall hear*
2	,, ,,	+**ēs**	**audi-ēs**	*You will hear*
3	,, ,,	+**et**	**audi-et**	*He will hear*
Plur. 1	,, ,,	+**ēmus**	**audi-ēmus**	*We shall hear*
2	,, ,,	+**ētis**	**audi-ētis**	*You will hear*
3	,, ,,	+**ent**	**audi-ent**	*They will hear*

In the Imperfect and Future the Personal Endings are the same as those of the Third Conjugation, but in the Present they are slightly different. Write out the Future Simple of **Reg-ō** and **Audi-ō** to show the difference.

VOCABULARY

Verbs of the Fourth Conjugation like **audi-ō**

Ērudi-ō, *I instruct*   **Pūni-ō,** *I punish*
Impedi-ō, *I hinder*   **Sci-ō,** *I know*
Mūr-us, -ī, m., *a wall*   **Verb-um, -ī,** n., *a word*
Ager, agrī, m., *a field*

EXERCISE XIV

    s.   o.   v.t.
1. Amīcus bonus fīlium meum ērudi-t.
2. Mūrī magni nūntiōs nostrōs impedi-ēbant.
3. Magister noster puerōs nōn pūni-et.
4. Servōs nostrōs et fīlium tuum ērudī-mus.
5. Rēgīna pulchra servum miserum nōn pūni-t.
6. Mūrus magnus et aqua nūntium impedi-ent.
7. Puer parvus multa verba sci-t.
8. Amicī nostrī agrōs magnōs habe-nt.
9. Puella pulchra magna dōna laudāv-erit.
10. Magistrī tuī multōs librōs sci-unt.
11. Sagittas et hastās longās timu-imus.
12. Puellās tenerās et puerōs parvōs ērudī-tis.

1. The long spears were hindering the little boys.
2. Good masters will instruct our sons.
3. The great queen does not punish the slaves.
4. You do not instruct the boys and girls.
5. The great wall hinders our messengers.
6. Many arrows had wounded the wretched queen.
7. Your friends will praise our fields.
8. The tender girls will know my words.
9. Our words will instruct the little girl.
10. We shall have sent books and many gifts.
11. The wretched girl will not avoid the danger.
12. I shall punish my son and your slaves.

Fourth Conjugation : Ī-Verbs—*continued*
Audī-re, *to hear*
Present Stem, audī-   *Perfect Stem,* audīv-
ACTIVE VOICE
TENSES FROMED FROM THE PERFECT STEM Audīv-

The Perfect Stem of a regular Verb of the Fourth Conjugation may be found by adding **v** to the Present Stem; thus—

Present Stem, audī-   *Perfect Stem,* audīv-

[The Personal Endings are the same in all Conjugations]

PERFECT AND AORIST				
	FORMATION	EXAMPLE	ENGLISH	
			Perfect	Aorist
	Perf. Stem			
Sing. 1	+ī	audīv-ī	*I have heard*	*I heard*
2	+istī	audīv-istī	*You have heard*	*You heard*
3	+it	audīv-it	*He has heard*	*He heard*
Plur. 1	+imus	audīv-imus	*We have heard*	*We heard*
2	+istis	audīv-istis	*You have heard*	*You heard*
3	+ērunt	audīv-ērunt	*They have heard*	*They heard*
	or +ēre	*or* audīv-ēre		
PLUPERFECT				
	Perf. Stem			
Sing. 1	+eram	audīv-eram	*I had heard*	
2	+erās	audīv-erās	*You had heard*	
3	+erat	audīv-erat	*He had heard*	
Plur. 1	+erāmus	audīv-erāmus	*We had heard*	
2	+erātis	audīv-erātis	*You had heard*	
3	+erant	audīv-erant	*They had heard*	
FUTURE PERFECT				
	Perf. Stem			
Sing. 1	+erō	audīv-erō	*I shall have heard*	
2	+eris	audīv-eris	*You will have heard*	
3	+erit	audīv-erit	*He will have heard*	
Plur. 1	+erimus	audīv-erimus	*We shall have heard*	
2	+eritis	audīv-eritis	*You will have heard*	
3	+erint	audīv-erint	*They will have heard*	

RULE.—**The Genitive Case shows to whom a thing belongs ;** thus, **Puerī liber,** *the boy's book,* or, *the book of the boy.*

VOCABULARY

Claud-ō (3), *I shut*	*Present Stem*, **claud-**	*Perfect Stem*, **claus-**
Frang-ō (3), *I break*	„ **frang-**	„ **frēg-**
Port-a, -ae, f., *a gate*		
Oppid-um, -ī, n., *a town*		

EXERCISE XV

1. Rēgīnae fīlius pugna-t.
2. Servī amīcus time-t.
3. Puerī librum tenē-s.
4. Iūliae verba laud-ō.
5. Servōrum tēla vola-nt.
6. Oppidī portam claud-ēs.
7. Puerī hastās frēg-ī.
8. Puellārum īram time-ō.
9. Magistrī fīlium dūc-it.
10. Magistrī puerōs doce-nt.
11. Rēgīna nostra servōs pūnīv-erit.
12. Magistrī bonī multōs puerōs ērudīv-erant.
13. Multās sagittās et hastās vītāv-ērunt.
14. Amīcus tuus nūntiōrum verba sci-t.
15. Servus niger oppidī portās claus-erit.
16. Rēgīnae fīliōs et servōs ērudīv-istī.
17. Hastās longās et sagittās frēg-erāmus.
18. Mūrī magnī nūntium tuum impedīv-erant.

1. We shall shut the great gate of the town.
2. The sons of the queen had broken many arrows.
3. The wall of the town will have hindered our messenger.
4. You have praised the gifts of the girls.
5. Our friends have many books.
6. The black slave was leading the little girl.
7. You have not shut the gate of the town.
8. The slaves held many arrows and spears.
9. We shall instruct the little son of the slave.
10. They had avoided the dangers of war.
11. We do not fear the slaves' words.
12. You have broken the gates and the great wall.

D

TABLE OF THE FOUR CONJUGATIONS

ACTIVE VOICE

		SINGULAR			PLURAL		
		1	2	3	1	2	3
Present	Amā-	ō[1]	s	t	mus	tis	nt
	Monē-	ō	s	t	mus	tis	nt
	Reg-	ō	is	it	imus	itis	unt
	Audī-	ō	s	t	mus	tis	unt
Imperfect	Amā- Monē- Reg- Audī-	bam ēbam	bās ēbās	bat ēbat	bāmus ēbāmus	bātis ēbātis	bant ēbant
Future Simple	Amā- Monē- Reg- Audī-	bō am	bis ēs	bit et	bimus ēmus	bitis ētis	bunt ent
Perfect & Aorist	Amāv- Monu- Rēx- Audīv-	ī	istī	it	imus	istis	ērunt or ēre
Pluperfect	Amav- Monu- Rex- Audīv-	eram	erās	erat	erāmus	erātis	erant
Future Perfect	Amāv- Monu- Rēx- Audīv-	erō	eris	erit	erimus	eritis	erint

ENGLISH

Present—*I love, am loving, do love*, **etc.**
Imperfect—*I was loving, etc.*
Future Simple—*I shall love, etc.*
Perfect—*I have loved, etc.*
Aorist—*I loved or did love, etc.*
Pluperfect—*I had loved.*
Future Perfect—*I shall have loved.*

---

[1] The First Person Singular Present is **amō** for **amāō**.

RECAPITULATORY

Active Voice, Four Conjugations

1. Ērudīv-erant.	13. Dūx-erimus.	25. Tene-nt.
2. Pugnā-s.	14. Claus-eris.	26. Claud-ēbātis.
3. Scrīps-erint.	15. Vocāv-erās.	27. Sci-ētis.
4. Docē-s.	16. Mitt-unt.	28. Mīs-imus.
5. Mīs-ērunt.	17. Terrē-tis.	29. Laudā-bit.
6. Vīta-t.	18. Frēg-istī.	30. Tenu-eram.
7. Rogā-bō.	19. Docu-eritis.	31. Habē-mus.
8. Impedi-ēs.	20. Vulnerā-tis.	32. Scrīb-am.
9. Habu-erat.	21. Frang-itis.	33. Claus-it.
10. Volā-bant.	22. Ērudi-ēmus.	34. Terru-erō.
11. Timu-imus.	23. Vītāv-istis.	35. Ērudī-tis.
12. Saltā-bis.	24. Cantā-bāmus.	36. Pūni-ent.

1. You (*sing.*) call.	13. We are writing.
2. We shall hold.	14. You (*pl.*) dance.
3. You were leading.	15. We have broken.
4. They will have sent.	16. You (*sing.*) have.
5. I had feared.	17. You (*pl.*) did not fear.
6. You (*pl.*) are teaching.	18. We taught.
7. They punish.	19. I shall send.
8. We do not ask.	20. You (*sing.*) punish.
9. I shall shut.	21. He wounds.
10. You (*sing.*) avoided.	22. You (*pl.*) were praising.
11. You (*pl.*) had had.	23. You (*sing.*) will hinder.
12. You (*sing.*) will have known.	24. You (*pl.*) lead.

NOUNS

THIRD DECLENSION

Nouns whose Genitive Singular ends in **is** belong to the Third Declension. The Nominative ending is various, and Nouns of all three Genders belong to the Third Declension. The Third Declension has two divisions—

1. Nouns which increase; that is, which have more syllables in the Genitive Singular than in the Nominative Singular.[1]
2. Nouns which do not increase; that is, which have the same number of syllables in the Genitive Singular as in the Nominative Singular.[2]

I. INCREASING NOUNS

MASCULINE AND FEMININE

SINGULAR			PLURAL	
Nom.	Iūdex	a judge (m.)	Iūdic-ēs	judges
Voc.	Iūdex	O judge	Iūdic-ēs	O judges
Acc.	Iūdic-em	a judge	Iūdic-ēs	judges
Gen.	Iūdic-is	of a judge	Iūdic-um	of judges
Dat.	Iūdic-ī	to or for a judge	Iūdic-ibus	to or for judges
Abl.	Iūdic-e	by, with, or from a judge[3]	Iūdic-ibus	by, with, or from judges
Nom.	Virgō	a maiden	Virgin-ēs	maidens
Voc.	Virgō	O maiden	Virgin-ēs	O maidens
Acc.	Virgin-em	a maiden	Virgin-ēs	maidens
Gen.	Virgin-is	of a maiden	Virgin-um	of maidens
Dat.	Virgin-ī	to or for a maiden	Virgin-ibus	to or for maidens
Abl.	Virgin-e	by, with, or from a maiden[3]	Virgin-ibus	by, with, or from maidens[3]

Observe that the Nominative and Vocative Singular is **iūdex**, but that all the other cases are formed by adding certain endings to the stem **iūdic-**; this stem is found by taking away **-is** from the Genitive Singular.

---

[1] These are called Imparisyllabic.   [2] These are called Parisyllabic.
[3] Require a Preposition for this meaning.

VOCABULARY

Words of the Third Declension, Genitive Plural -**um**

Decline—

Rēx, rēg-is, m., *a king*   **Mīles, mīlit-is**, m., *a soldier*
Vōx, vōc-is, f., *a voice*   **Leō, leōn-is**, m., *a lion*

EXERCISE XVI

1. Iūdic-ēs scrīb-ēbant.
2. Mīlit-em timu-imus.
3. Rēg-ēs pugnāv-ērunt.
4. Rēg-is vōc-em aud-iō.
5. Leōn-ēs vītā-bis.
6. Rēg-em vocāv-istī.
7. Vōx rēg-is terre-t.
8. Puer leōn-em time-t.
9. Mīlit-ēs pugnāv-erant.
10. Rēg-um fīliōs docē-s.
11. Virgin-em laudā-bās.
12. Iūdex sci-et.
13. Mīlit-ēs vōc-em rēg-is nōn audīv-ērunt.
14. Puerī parvī leōn-em vulnerāv-erant.
15. Mīlit-um hastās longās frēg-imus.
16. Rēg-is amīcī multōs nūntiōs mīs-erant.
17. Puella tenera leōn-is vōc-em timē-bat.
18. Vōx tua puerōs parvōs terru-it.

1. The soldiers will fight.
2. The kings had praised.
3. We heard a voice.
4. You (*pl.*) feared the lions.
5. You (*s.*) love the king.
6. The judges punish.
7. I praised the maiden.
8. I call the king's slaves.
9. The judge's son sings.
10. You (*pl.*) taught kings.
11. The sons of the king had written many letters.
12. The judges punished the slaves and the soldiers.
13. The boys' spears had wounded the lion.
14. Your voice will frighten the little girls.
15. The soldiers avoided the spears of the slaves.
16. We do not hear the maiden's words.
17. The king and the queen will praise the soldiers.

Third Declension—*continued*

I. INCREASING NOUNS

NEUTER

Remember that all Neuter Nouns have Nominative, Vocative, and Accusative alike, and that in the Plural the Nominative, Vocative, and Accusative end in **a**.

	SINGULAR			PLURAL	
Nom.	**Nōmen**	*a name (n.)*	**Nōmin-a**	*names*	
Voc.	**Nōmen**	*O name*	**Nōmin-a**	*O names*	
Acc.	**Nōmen**	*a name*	**Nōmin-a**	*names*	
Gen.	**Nōmin-is**	*of a name*	**Nōmin-um**	*of names*	
Dat.	**Nōmin-ī**	*to or for a name*	**Nōmin-ibus**	*to or for names*	
Abl.	**Nōmin-e**	*by, with, or from a name*	**Nōmin-ibus**	*by, with, or from names*	
Nom.	**Opus**	*work (n.)*	**Oper-a**	*works*	
Voc.	**Opus**	*O work*	**Oper-a**	*O works*	
Acc.	**Opus**	*work*	**Oper-a**	*works*	
Gen.	**Oper-is**	*of work*	**Oper-um**	*of works*	
Dat.	**Oper-i**	*to or for work*	**Oper-ibus**	*to or for works*	
Abl.	**Oper-e**	*by, with, or from work*	**Oper-ibus**	*by, with, or from works*	

In making an Adjective like **bonus** or **niger** agree with a Noun of the Third Declension, remember that the Adjective is declined like the Second or First Declension while the Noun is of the Third Declension; therefore the endings of the Adjective will not always be the same as those of the Noun; thus, **Rēgēs bonī**, *good kings.*

Decline together **Rēx magnus—vōx tua—onus parvum**.

VOCABULARY

Neuter words of Third Declension, Genitive Plural **-um**

Decline—

Carmen, carmin-is, n., *a song*   Onus, oner-is, n., *a burden*

Flūmen, flūmin-is, n., *a river*

EXERCISE XVII

	s.	o.	v.t.

1. Puellae pulchrae multa carmin-a cantā-bant.
2. Flūmen magnum mīlit-ēs nostrōs terrē-bit.
3. Rēg-is servī onus magnum timu-ērunt.
4. Iūdic-ēs bonī mīlit-em miserum pūni-ent.
5. Mīlit-ēs nostrī portās magnās claus-ērunt.
6. Rēg-em magnum et rēgīnam amā-bimus.
7. Flūmina magna nūntiōs meōs impedīv-erant.
8. Virgin-ēs pulchrae carmen longum canta-nt.
9. Iūdic-is bonī verba audi-ēmus.
10. Multōrum mīlit-um hastās frēg-erātis.
11. Virgō tenera onus magnum tenē-bat.
12. Servī nostrī onera magna portā-bant.

1. The great kings punished the wretched slaves.
2. We heard the voices of many soldiers.
3. Your voice will frighten the son of the queen.
4. The king and the queen praised the good judge.
5. You heard the songs of the beautiful girls.
6. Many soldiers were holding arrows and spears.
7. The great river will hinder our slaves.
8. We had led the little son of the great king.
9. The son of the good judge has many books.
10. The slaves had shut the great gates of our town.
11. The good king praised the song of the girls.
12. The little boys feared the voice of the great lion.

Third Declension—*continued*

II. NON-INCREASING NOUNS

Nouns that do not increase (see p. 42) form their Genitive Plural in **-ium** instead of **um.**[1] In all the other Cases the endings are the same as those of Increasing Nouns.

FEMININE

	SINGULAR		PLURAL	
Nom.	Ov-is	a sheep (f.)	Ov-ēs	sheep
Voc.	Ov-is	O sheep	Ov-ēs	O sheep
Acc.	Ov-em	a sheep	Ov-ēs	sheep
Gen.	Ov-is	of a sheep	Ov-ium	of sheep
Dat.	Ov-ī	to or for a sheep	Ov-ibus	to or for sheep
Abl.	Ov-e	by, with, or from a sheep	Ov-ibus	by, with, or from sheep

NEUTER

	SINGULAR		PLURAL	
Nom.	Cubĭl-e	a bed (n.)	Cubĭl-ia	beds
Voc.	Cubĭl-e	O bed	Cubĭl-ia	O beds
Acc.	Cubĭl-e	a bed	Cubĭl-ia	beds
Gen.	Cubĭl-is	of a bed	Cubĭl-ium	of beds
Dat.	Cubĭl-ī	to or for a bed	Cubĭl-ibus	to or for beds
Abl.	Cubĭl-ī	by, with, or from a bed	Cubĭl-ibus	by, with, or from beds

Decline together **Avis parva, mare magnum.**

---

[1] The rule is here given absolutely, to avoid confusion. Wherever in the following exercises exceptional Nouns have been used the Genitive Plural has been avoided.

VOCABULARY

Words of the Third Declension, Genitive Plural **-ium**

Av-is, -is, f., *a bird*　　　　**Host-is, -is,** c., *an enemy* [1]
Nāv-is, -is, f., *a ship*　　　　**Mar-e, -is,** n., *a sea*
Vinc-ō (3), *I conquer*　　*Present Stem,* **vinc-**　　*Perfect Stem,* **vic-**

EXERCISE XVIII

      s.   o.   v. t.

1. Rēgis mīlitēs multōs hostēs vīc-ērunt.
2. Rēgīna nostra nāvem magnam mitt-et.
3. Ovēs tenerae leōnem magnum timē-bant.
4. Hostium sagittae rēgem vestrum vulnera-nt.
5. Avis parva vōcem tuam timu-erat.
6. Avium parvārum carmina audīv-imus.
7. Navēs magnās et multōs mīlitēs dūc-is.
8. Rēgis fīlius hostium tēla nōn timu-it.
9. Mare magnum multās puellās terre-t.
10. Mīlitum tēla mūrōs nostrōs nōn frang-ent.
11. Epistulās longās et librōs multōs scrīps-ī.
12. Rēgīnae fīlius cubīle parvum habe-t.

1. The king's ships will avoid our enemies.
2. The girls heard the voices of the little birds.
3. We do not fear the great ship of our enemies.
4. The darts of the soldiers wounded many slaves.
5. Your enemies will not conquer the queen's soldiers.
6. The little boy was holding a beautiful bird.
7. Your arrows have wounded the tender sheep.
8. We praise the voice of the beautiful maiden.
9. You (*pl.*) had broken the spears of many soldiers.
10. The ships of the enemy frightened our slaves.
11. You (*s.*) have not shut the great gates of your town.
12. The judges do not fear the dangers of the sea.

---

[1] **Hostis** may, of course, be Feminine.

THE VERB 'SUM'

Present Stem, **es-**   *Perfect Stem,* **fu-**

The Verb **sum** belongs to none of the Four Conjugations, and is irregular in Present Stem Tenses.

PRESENT			PERFECT AND AORIST		
Sing. 1	sum	*I am*	fu-ī	*I have been*	*I was*
2	es	*You are*	fu-istī	*You have been*	*You were*
3	est	*He is*	fu-it	*He has been*	*He was*
Plur. 1	sumus	*We are*	fu-imus	*We have been*	*We were*
2	estis	*You are*	fu-istis	*You have been*	*You were*
3	sunt	*They are*	fu-ērunt	*They have*	*They*
			or fu-ēre	*been*	*were*

IMPERFECT			PLUPERFECT		
Sing. 1	eram	*I was*	fu-eram	*I had been*	
2	erās	*You were*	fu-erās	*You had been*	
3	erat	*He was*	fu-erat	*He had been*	
Plur. 1	erāmus	*We were*	fu-erāmus	*We had been*	
2	erātis	*You were*	fu-erātis	*You had been*	
3	erant	*They were*	fu-erant	*They had been*	

FUTURE			FUTURE PERFECT		
Sing. 1	erō	*I shall be*	fu-erō	*I shall have been*	
2	eris	*You will be*	fu-eris	*You will have been*	
3	erit	*He will be*	fu-erit	*He will have been*	
Plur. 1	erimus	*We shall be*	fu-erimus	*We shall have been*	
2	eritis	*You will be*	fu-eritis	*You will have been*	
3	erunt	*They will be*	fu-erint	*They will have been*	

The Verb **sum** is a Copulative Verb, that is, it joins the Subject to another word which may be a Noun or an Adjective, and is called the Complement. See pages 1 and 3.

RULE.—**The Complement agrees with the Subject.**

S.   V.C.   C.
Rēgīna   est   bona = *the queen is good*

Here **bona** is the Complement, and is Nominative Case Singular, and Feminine Gender, to agree with **rēgīna**.

(In the Analysis V.C. = Verb Copulative, C. = Complement.)

VOCABULARY

Dūr-us, -a, -um, *hard*   Alt-us, -a, -um, *high, deep*
Timid-us, -a, -um, *timid*   Aeger, aegra, aegrum, *sick*
Dēns-us, -a, -um, *thick*

EXERCISE XIX

s.   v.c.   c.
1. Puella est pulchra.
2. Avēs erant pulchrae.
3. Servus erit nūntius.
4. Rēx fu-it timidus.
5. Cubīle fu-erat dūrum.
6. Avis fu-erit parva.
7. Rēgēs sunt magnī.
8. Mūrī erunt altī.
9. Ovēs fu-ērunt parvae.

s.   c.   v.c.
10. Fīlius bonus erat.
11. Portae dēnsae fu-erint.
12. Hostēs multī fu-erant.
13. Amīcī sumus.
14. Mīlitēs estis.
15. Miserī eritis.
16. Aegrī fu-istis.
17. Servus eris.
18. Rēgīna fu-erās.

19. Fīlius servī tuī est nūntius noster.
20. Mīlitēs rēgīnae nostrae multī sunt.
21. Portae oppidī vestrī magnae erant.

1. The king was sick.
2. The bed was small.
3. The ships are great.
4. The gifts will be many.
5. Your son is a slave.
6. We had been friends.
7. You will have been sick.
8. We are not soldiers.
9. The words were good.
10. You have been a king.
11. The letter will be long.
12. We are the king's sons.
13. The friends of the queen are the enemies of the king.
14. The gates of the great town will be high.
15. The spears of our soldiers were hard.
16. The beds of the little boys were not long.
17. The enemies of your king were timid.
18. The son of your friend had been our slave.

FIRST CONJUGATION : Ā-VERBS

Amā-re, *to love*

Pres. Stem, **amā-**   *Perf. Stem,* **amāv-**   *Sup. Stem,* **amāt-**

PASSIVE VOICE

TENSES FORMED FROM PRESENT STEM **Amā-**

PRESENT			
	FORMATION	EXAMPLE	ENGLISH
Sing. 1	Pres. Stem +or	am-or [1]	*I am loved*
2	,, ,, +ris	amā-ris	*You are loved*
3	,, ,, +tur	amā-tur	*He is loved*
Plur. 1	,, ,, +mur	amā-mur	*We are loved*
2	,, ,, +minī	amā-minī	*You are loved*
3	,, ,, +ntur	ama-ntur	*They are loved*
IMPERFECT			
Sing. 1	Pres. Stem +bar	amā-bar	*I was being loved*
2	,, ,, +bāris	amā-bāris	*You were being loved*
3	,, ,, +bātur	amā-bātur	*He was being loved*
Plur. 1	,, ,, +bāmur	amā-bāmur	*We were being loved*
2	,, ,, +bāminī	amā-bāminī	*You were being loved*
3	,, ,, +bantur	amā-bantur	*They were being loved*
FUTURE SIMPLE			
Sing. 1	Pres. Stem +bor	amā-bor	*I shall be loved*
2	,, ,, +beris	amā-beris	*You will be loved*
3	,, ,, +bitur	amā-bitur	*He will be loved*
Plur. 1	,, ,, +bimur	amā-bimur	*We shall be loved*
2	,, ,, +biminī	amā-biminī	*You will be loved*
3	,, ,, +buntur	amā-buntur	*They will be loved*

[The Impf. and Fut. Simple have each another form for the Second Person Singular, viz. Impf. **amā-bāre**, Fut. **amā-bere**.]

N.B.—Only Transitive Verbs have a complete Passive Voice, but when turned into the Passive Voice they become Intransitive, and cannot therefore have an Object.

---

[1] **Am-or** is for **amā-or**, just as the Active **am-ō** is for **amā-ō**.

VOCABULARY

Pōrt-o (1), *I carry*   **Culp-ō** (1), *I blame*
Mōnstr-ō (1), *I show, point out*   **Turr-is, -is,** f., *a tower*

EXERCISE XX

1. Laudā-bitur.
2. Culpā-bāmur.
3. Onus portā-tur.
4. Puerī culpa-ntur.
5. Nōn vocā-beris.
6. Mōnstrā-buntur.
7. Vulnerā-bāminī.
8. Aqua portā-bitur.
9. Nōn culpā-mur.
10. Vulnerā-biminī.
11. Rēx mōnstrā-bātur.
12. Vocā-bāris.

13. Fīliī tuī et amīcus noster laudā-buntur.
14. Turrēs altae oppidī nostrī mōnstra-ntur.
15. Multī mīlitēs hastās et sagittās frēg-erant.
16. Nāvēs rēgis nostrī hostem timidum terrē-bunt.
17. Iūdic-is fīlius et servus meus culpā-bantur.
18. Puellae timidae leōnem magnum timu-ērunt.

[Remember that the Active Voice expresses what the Subject of a Verb is or does.
The Passive Voice expresses what is done to the Subject of the Verb. Thus, *The boy calls* (Active); *the boy is called* (Passive).]

1. We are blamed.
2. You were being praised.
3. They will be carried.
4. You are not fearing.
5. We were singing.
6. He was being blamed.
7. The voice is praised.
8. The boy is calling.
9. The girls are called.
10. You will be blamed.
11. You are avoiding.
12. We were being called.

13. The great burdens of our slaves were being carried.
14. The voice of the beautiful maiden will be praised.
15. The timid soldiers of the king are not praised.
16. The gates and the towers of the town will be shown.
17. You are blaming the friends of the good judges.
18. The letters and books of your friend will be shown.

First Conjugation : Ā-Verbs—*continued*

Amā-re, *to love*

Pres. Stem, **amā-**   Perf. Stem, **amāv-**   Sup. Stem, **amāt-**

PASSIVE VOICE

TENSES FORMED FROM SUPINE STEM **Amāt-**

These Tenses are made up of the Participle **amāt-us** and Tenses of **sum.**

The Supine Stem of a Regular Verb of the First Conjugation is found by adding **t** to the Present Stem.

			PERFECT AND AORIST		
	FORMATION	EXAMPLE	ENGLISH		
			Perfect	Aorist	
Sing. 1	Supine Stem +us sum	amāt-us sum	*I have been*	*I was*	
2	+us es	amāt-us es	*You have been*	*You were*	
3	+us est	amāt-us est	*He has been*	*He was*	
Plur. 1	+ī sumus	amātī- sumus	*We have been*	*We were*	
2	+ī estis	amāt-ī estis	*You have been*	*You were*	
3	+ī sunt	amāt-ī sunt	*They have been*	*They were*	

(Perfect column bracketed: *loved*; Aorist column bracketed: *loved*)

The Participle **amāt-us** used in forming this Tense has three Terminations for the three Genders, like an Adjective ending in **-us, -a, -um,** and it must, like an Adjective, agree in Gender and Number with the Subject of the Verb ; thus—

SING.
- *Masculine* **Puer amāt-us est** = *the boy was loved*
- *Feminine* **Virgō amāt-a est** = *the maiden was loved*
- *Neuter* **Nōmen amāt-um est** = *the name was loved*

PLUR.
- *Masculine* **Puerī amāt-ī sunt** = *the boys were loved*
- *Feminine* **Virginēs amāt-ae sunt** = *the maidens were loved*
- *Neuter* **Nōmina amāt-a sunt** = *the names were loved*

VOCABULARY

Lēx, lēg-is, f., *a law*   Lapis, lapid-is, m., *a stone*

EXERCISE XXI

    v.p.   s.

1. Laudāt-ī estis.
2. Nāvēs mōnstrāt-ae sunt.
3. Onus portāt-um est.
4. Rēgēs culpāt-ī sunt.
5. Vulnerāt-ī sumus.

    s.   v.p.

6. Virgō vocāt-a est.
7. Mīlitēs sunt timidī.
8. Vulnerāt-us sum.
9. Oppidum est magnum.
10. Rēgis fīliī estis.

11. Lēgēs bonae rēgum nostrōrum laudāt-ae sunt.
12. Portae altae oppidī magnī mōnstrāt-ae sunt.
13. Rēgīnae fīlius parvus vulnerāt-us est.
14. Opus puellārum pulchrārum laudāt-um est.
15. Multa flūmina hostēs nostrōs impedi-ent.
16. Multōs mīlitēs et nāvēs magnās mīs-istī.
17. Carmina virginis pulchrae laudāt-a sunt.
18. Multī mīlitēs et rēx magnus vulnerāt-ī sunt.

[*N.B.*—' I *was* loved ' is the Aorist Passive.
   ' I *was being* loved ' is the Imperfect Passive.
   ' I *was* loving ' is the Imperfect Active.]

1. You were called.
2. We were blamed.
3. The work was praised.
4. The girl has been called.
5. The girls were beautiful.

6. We were being called.
7. Boys were fighting.
8. Kings were wounded.
9. The voice was praised.
10. Spears were carried.

11. The song of the beautiful maidens was praised.
12. The great ships of our kings were shown.
13. The soldiers of the good queen have been wounded.
14. The messengers of the judges will be blamed.
15. The great stones of the walls were being shown.
16. We do not fear the ships and soldiers of the enemy.
17. You have written many letters and many books.
18. The gifts of the little boys were praised.

First Conjugation : Ā-Verbs—*continued*

Amā-re, *to love*

Pres. Stem, **amā-**   Perf. Stem, **amāv-**   Sup. Stem, **amāt-**

PASSIVE VOICE

TENSES FORMED FROM THE SUPINE STEM **Amāt-**

		FORMATION	EXAMPLE	ENGLISH
		PLUPERFECT		
Sing.	1	Supine Stem +us eram	amāt-us eram	*I had been loved*
	2	+us erās	amāt-us erās	*You had been loved*
	3	+us erat	amāt-us erat	*He had been loved*
Plur.	1	+ī erāmus	amāt-ī erāmus	*We had been loved*
	2	+ī erātis	amāt-ī erātis	*You had been loved*
	3	+ī erant	amāt-ī erant	*They had been loved*
		FUTURE PERFECT		
Sing.	1	Supine Stem +us erō	amāt-us erō	*I shall have been loved*
	2	+us eris	amāt-us eris	*You will have been loved*
	3	+us erit	amāt-us erit	*He will have been loved*
Plur.	1	+ī erimus	amāt-ī erimus	*We shall have been loved*
	2	+ī eritis	amāt-ī eritis	*You will have been loved*
	3	+ī erunt	amāt-ī erunt	*They will have been loved*

N.B.—In the above Tenses, as in the Perfect Tense, the Participle must agree in Gender and Number with the Subject. See page 52.

ABLATIVE OF INSTRUMENT AND AGENT

The Thing with which an action is done is called the Instrument. and is put in the Ablative; thus, **Sagittīs vulnerāt-us est**=*he was wounded (by) with arrows* (Ablative of Instrument *without* Preposition).

The Person by whom an action is done is called the Agent, and when the Verb is Passive the Agent is put in the Ablative with the Preposition **a** or **ab**; thus, **Ā mīlite vulnerāt-us est**=*he was wounded by the soldier* (Ablative of Agent).

RULE—' By ' (or ' with ') a *Thing*—Ablative only.
      ' By ' a *Person* or *Animal*—Ablative with ' a ' or ' ab.'

VOCABULARY

Oppugn-ō (1), *I attack*   **Aedific-ō** (1), *I build*

EXERCISE XXII

[*N.B.*—ā and **ab** both mean ' by,' but ā is used before consonants, **ab** before vowels and **h**.]

1. Virginēs pulchrae ā rēge magnō laudāt-ae sunt.
2. Multī mīlitēs sagittīs vestrīs oppugnāt-ī erant.
3. Multa onera ā servīs miserīs portāt-a erunt.
4. Perīculum magnum ā mīlitibus vītāt-um erat.
5. Hastīs et sagittīs hostium vulnerāt-ī erāmus.
6. Ab amicīs rēgīnae bonae culpāt-us eris.
7. Mīlitēs portās lapide magnō frēg-ērunt.
8. Rēgis servī mūrum altum aedificāv-ērunt.
9. Rēgīna nostra ā mīlitibus amāt-a erat.
10. Avis tenera ā puerō lapide vulnerāt-a est.
11. Multa carmina ā puellīs pulchrīs canta-ntur.
12. Virginēs timidae aquam flūminis timu-ērunt.

1. The good boys will be praised by the masters.
2. The king has been wounded by the arrows of the slaves.
3. Your books had been praised by the friends of the judges.
4. The tender girl had been wounded by a great stone.
5. Many rivers will have been pointed out by the boys.
6. We have been blamed by the king and by the queen.
7. You will have been called by our friends.
8. We shall break the gates of the town with our spears.
9. You have frightened the timid girls with your voice.
10. Many towns were attacked by the soldiers.
11. We were building a high wall with great stones.
12. The judges have written great books and many letters.

E

ADJECTIVES OF THIRD DECLENSION

Besides the Adjectives in $\left\{ \begin{array}{l} \text{-us, -a, -um,} \\ \text{-er, -a, -um,} \end{array} \right\}$ which follow the First and Second Declensions, there are others which follow the Third Declension of Nouns.

The Adjectives declined below have one form for the Masculine and Feminine Gender and another for the Neuter in Nominative, Vocative, and Accusative; in the other Cases they have the same form for all Genders.

Melior = *better*

	SINGULAR		PLURAL	
	Masc. or Fem.	Neut.	Masc. or Fem.	Neut.
Nom.	Melior	melius	Meliōr-ēs	meliōr-a
Voc.	Melior	melius	Meliōr-ēs	meliōr-a
Acc.	Meliōr-em	melius	Meliōr-ēs	meliōr-a
Gen.	Meliōr-is	meliōr-is	Meliōr-um	meliōr-um
Dat.	Meliōr-ī	meliōr-ī	Meliōr-ibus	meliōr-ibus
Abl.	Meliōr-e	meliōr-e	Meliōr-ibus	meliōr-ibus

Trīstis = *sad*

	SINGULAR		PLURAL	
	Masc. or Fem.	Neut.	Masc. or Fem.	Neut.
Nom.	Trīst-is	trīst-e	Trīst-ēs	trīst-ia
Voc.	Trīst-is	trīst-e	Trīst-ēs	trīst-ia
Acc.	Trīst-em	trīst-e	Trīst-ēs	trīst-ia
Gen.	Trīst-is	trīst-is	Trīst-ium	trīst-ium
Dat.	Trīst-ī	trīst-ī	Trīst-ibus	trīst-ibus
Abl.	Trīst-ī	trīst-ī	Trīst-ibus	trīst-ibus

Observe that the Ablative Singular ends in ī, not ē.

Decline together **Dōnum melius—hasta gravis—servus fortis—onus leve—fīlius melior—tēlum grave.**

VOCABULARY

Decline like **trīstis**—

Fortis, *brave* **Gravis,** *heavy*
Brevis, *short* **Dulcis,** *sweet*

EXERCISE XXIII

1. Rēx est fortis.
2. Onus erat grave.
3. Carmina sunt dulcia.
4. Hasta brevis erit.
5. Puerī fortēs erant.
6. Vōx dulcis fuit.
7. Carminum dulcium.
8. Sagittīs brevibus.
9. Ā mīlite fortī.
10. Opus erat melius.
11. Rēgis fīliī carmen dulce cantā-bant.
12. Onera gravia ā servīs miserīs portāt-a sunt.
13. Rēgīna nostra ā mīlitibus fortibus amāt-a erat.
14. Epistulae puerōrum parvōrum sunt brevēs.
15. Mīlitum fortium hastās gravēs timē-mus.
16. Avium parvārum vōcem dulcem laudāv-istī.
17. Amīcī nostrī dōna meliōra mitt-ent.
18. Iūdicis fīlius sagittā brevī vulnerāt-us est.

1. The song was short.
2. The girls are brave.
3. The books were heavy.
4. Of brave soldiers.
5. By a short spear.
6. By brave boys.
7. Of a sweet song.
8. Short letters.
9. A better gift.
10. Of better spears.
11. The sweet voices of the girls will lead our friends.
12. We were wounded by the heavy spears of the soldiers.
13. The heavy books were carried by the little boys.
14. The short song had been praised by the king.
15. The arrows of the brave soldiers are short.
16. The heavy stones will hinder the king's messengers.
17. Better ships will be built by the brave queen.
18. The wretched slaves will fear the heavy burdens.

Adjectives of Third Declension—*continued*

The Adjectives declined below have in the Accusative Singular, and Nominative, Vocative, and Accusative Plural, one form for Masculine and Feminine and another for the Neuter, but in all the other Cases they have the same form for all three Genders.

Fēlīx = *happy*

	SINGULAR		PLURAL	
	Masc. or Fem.	Neut.	Masc. or Fem.	Neut.
Nom.	Fēlīx	fēlīx	Fēlīc-ēs	fēlīc-ia
Voc.	Fēlīx	fēlīx	Fēlīc-ēs	fēlīc-ia
Acc.	Fēlīc-em	fēlīx	Fēlīc-ēs	fēlīc-ia
Gen.	Fēlīc-is	fēlīc-is	Fēlīc-ium	fēlīc-ium
Dat.	Fēlīc-ī	fēlīc-ī	Fēlīc-ibus	fēlīc-ibus
Abl.	Fēlīc-ī	fēlīc-ī	Fēlīc-ibus	fēlīc-ibus

Ingēns = *vast*

	SINGULAR		PLURAL	
	Masc. or Fem.	Neut.	Masc. or Fem.	Neut.
Nom.	Ingēns	ingēns	Ingent-ēs	ingent-ia
Voc.	Ingēns	ingēns	Ingent-ēs	ingent-ia
Acc.	Ingent-em	ingēns	Ingent-ēs	ingent-ia
Gen.	Ingent-is	ingent-is	Ingent-ium	ingent-ium
Dat.	Ingent-ī	ingent-ī	Ingent-ibus	ingent-ibus
Abl.	Ingent-ī	ingent-ī	Ingent-ibus	ingent-ibus

Decline together **Puella fēlīx**—**mare ingēns**—**magister sapiēns**—**tēlum vēlōx**—**servus audāx**—**dōnum ingēns**.

RULE.—A Noun is sometimes qualified by another Noun which agrees with it in Case, and is said to be in Apposition.
Thus—

Rōmulus rēx pugnāvit = *Romulus the king has fought.*
Rōmulum rēgem timēmus = *we fear Romulus the king.*
Fīlius Rōmulī rēgis = *the son of Romulus the king.*

VOCABULARY

Decline—

Like Fēlīx	Like Ingēns
Vēlōx, vēlōc-is, *swift*	Sapiēns, sapient-is, *wise*
Audāx, audāc-is, *bold*	

Gai-us, -ī, Caesar, -is, Lentul-us, -ī (*names of men*)

EXERCISE XXIV

1. Rēgēs sapientēs bella longa nōn ama-nt.
2. Lentulus, amīcus noster, puerum audācem pūni-et.
3. Nūntiī vēlōcēs librōs, dōna tua, portā-bant.
4. Servī sapientēs ā Gaiō magistrō laudāt-ī sunt.
5. Librōs et epistulās, Caesaris opera, laudā-mus.
6. Multae nāvēs ā rēgīnā sapientī aedificāt-ae sunt.
7. Gaius, iūdex bonus, sagittā brevī vulnerāt-us est.
8. Opera servōrum audācium ā rēge culpāt-a sunt.
9. Magistrī sapientis verba ā puerīs lauda-ntur.
10. Hastās vēlōcēs et lapidēs gravēs timē-mus.
11. Gaius et Caesar, amīcī nostrī, sagittīs vulnerāt-ī erant.
12. Lentulus, iūdicis fīlius, multōs librōs scrīps-it.

1. The bold slaves broke the heavy gates of the town.
2. Gaius, your friend, has been praised by the judge.
3. The vast walls were being built by the slaves of the queen.
4. The books of Gaius, the judge, were praised by the king.
5. We feared the swift arrows and the heavy spears.
6. They were hearing the voices of the wise judges.
7. Lentulus and Caesar, our friends, had been called.
8. The towns had been attacked by the bold slaves.
9. Gaius, our slave, has been wounded by a heavy stone.
10. A sweet song was sung by Julia, a happy girl.
11. The bold lion had terrified the tender sheep.
12. The son of the wise master had led the brave soldiers.

SECOND CONJUGATION : Ē-VERBS

Monē-re, *to advise*

Pres. Stem, **monē-** *Perf. Stem,* **monu-** *Sup. Stem,* **monit-**

PASSIVE VOICE

TENSES FORMED FROM PRESENT STEM **Monē-**

[The Personal Endings are the same as those of the First Conjugation]

		PRESENT		
	FORMATION	EXAMPLE	ENGLISH	
	Present Stem			
Sing. 1	+or	mone-or	*I am (being) advised*	
2	+ris	monē-ris	*You are advised*	
3	+tur	monē-tur	*He is advised*	
Plur. 1	+mur	monē-mur	*We are advised*	
2	+minī	monē-minī	*You are advised*	
3	+ntur	mone-ntur	*They are advised*	

		IMPERFECT		
	Present Stem			
Sing. 1	+bar	monē-bar	*I was being advised*	
2	+bāris	monē-bāris	*You were being advised*	
3	+bātur	monē-bātur	*He was being advised*	
Plur. 1	+bāmur	monē-bāmur	*We were being advised*	
2	+bāminī	monē-bāminī	*You were being advised*	
3	+bantur	monē-bantur	*They were being advised*	

		FUTURE SIMPLE		
	Present Stem			
Sing. 1	+bor	monē-bor	*I shall be advised*	
2	+beris	monē-beris	*You will be advised*	
3	+bitur	monē-bitur	*He will be advised*	
Plur. 1	+bimur	monē-bimur	*We shall be advised*	
2	+biminī	monē-biminī	*You will be advised*	
3	+buntur	monē-buntur	*They will be advised*	

[The Impf. and Fut. Simple have each another form for the Second Person Singular, viz. Impf. **monē-bāre**, Fut. **monē-bere**.]

VOCABULARY

Sor-or, -ōris, f., *a sister*   Rōm-a, -ae, f., *Rome*
Urbs, urb-is, f., *a city*   Gall-us, -ī, *a Gaul*

EXERCISE XXV

1. Iūlia, soror mea, ā servō nigrō terrē-bitur.
2. Leōnēs magnī ab ovibus tenerīs time-ntur.
3. Rōma, urbs magna, ab hostibus oppugnāt-a erat.
4. Multī puerī ā Gaiō, amīcō tuō, doce-ntur.
5. Iūdicis bonī verba sapientia audīv-imus.
6. Mīlitēs fortēs hostium sagittis nōn terrē-buntur.
7. Rōmulus, rēx sapiēns, portās urbis claus-erit.
8. Avēs timidae puerōrum vōcibus terrē-bantur.
9. Carmen dulce ā Iūliā, sorōre tuā, cantāt-um est.
10. Hostēs audācēs portās urbis nostrae frēg-erant.
11. Epistulae Lentulī, amīcī nostrī, laudāt-ae sunt.
12. Onera gravia ā servīs miserīs timē-bantur.

1. Gaius, the son of our friend, will lead the soldiers.
2. The boys were being taught by Lentulus, a wise master.
3. We do not fear Gaius, the son of a wise judge.
4. You were wounded by the heavy spears of the soldiers.
5. Julia, the sister of Gaius, your friend, is beautiful.
6. The little birds are frightened by our voices.
7. The bold enemy (*pl.*) will not attack the great city.
8. Your letters will have been praised by the wise queen.
9. You were being taught by Gaius, the son of our friend.
10. The king's words will be feared by your slaves.
11. The gates of the city were pointed out by the enemy.
12. The short spears of the enemy (*pl.*) wounded many soldiers.

Second Conjugation: Ē-Verbs—*continued*
Monē-re, *to advise*

Pres. Stem, monē-   *Perf. Stem,* monu-   *Sup. Stem,* monit-

PASSIVE VOICE

TENSES FORMED FROM THE SUPINE STEM Monit-[1]

PERFECT AND AORIST				
	FORMATION	EXAMPLE	ENGLISH	
			Perfect	Aorist
Sing. 1	Supine Stem +us sum	monit-us sum	I have been	I was
2	+us es	monit-us es	You have been	You were
3	+us est	monit-us est	He has been	He was
Plur. 1	+ī sumus	monit-ī sumus	We have been	We were
2	+ī estis	monit-ī estis	You have been	You were
3	+ī sunt	monit-ī sunt	They have been	They were

(right margin: advised ... advised)

PLUPERFECT			
Sing. 1	Supine Stem +us eram	monit-us eram	I had been advised
2	+us erās	monit-us erās	You had been advised
3	+us erat	monit-us erat	He had been advised
Plur. 1	+ī erāmus	monit-ī erāmus	We had been advised
2	+ī erātis	monit-ī erātis	You had been advised
3	+ī erant	monit-ī erant	They had been advised

FUTURE PERFECT			
Sing. 1	Supine Stem +us erō	monit-us erō	I shall have been advised
2	+us eris	monit-us eris	You will have been advised
3	+us erit	monit-us erit	He will have been advised
Plur. 1	+ī erimus	monit-ī erimus	We shall have been advised
2	+ī eritis	monit-ī eritis	You will have been advised
3	+ī erunt	monit-ī erunt	They will have been advised

RULE.—When an adjective qualifies two or more Nouns of different Genders the Adjective agrees with the Masculine rather than with the Feminine.

Puer et puella sunt pulchrī =*the boy and the girl are beautiful*

The same rule applies to the Participle used in the Perfect Stem Tenses of the Passive Voice.

Puer et puella laudātī sunt =*the boy and the girl were praised*

---

[1] Supine Stems of many Second Conjugation verbs are irregular, and should be looked up.

VOCABULARY

Doce-ō (2), *I teach*   *Perfect Stem*, **docu-**   *Supine Stem*, **doct-**
Vide-ō (2), *I see*   ,,   **vīd-**   ,,   **vīs-**
Move-ō (2), *I move*   ,,   **mōv-**   „   **mōt-**
Omnis (Adjective like **trīstis**), *all*

EXERCISE XXVI

1. Rēx et rēgīna ab omnibus mīlitibus vīs-ī sunt.
2. Fīlius tuus et soror mea ā magistrō bonō doct-ī erunt.
3. Flūmina magna et mūrī altī rēgem impedi-ent.
4. Mūrus et porta oppidī nostrī sunt altī.
5. Rōmam, urbem nostram, et Rōmulum rēgem amā-mus.
6. Verba sapientia iūdicum bonōrum nōn audīv-istī.
7. Multae avēs puerōrum sagittīs vulnerāt-ae sunt.
8. Onus magnum ā servīs timidīs nōn mōt-um erit.
9. Rōma, urbs nostra, ā Romulō rēge aedificāt-a est.
10. Virginēs pulchrae carmina dulcia cantā-bant.
11. Gaius, amīcus tuus, et Iūlia, soror mea, aegrī fu-ērunt.
12. Librī tuī ab omnibus amīcīs nostrīs laudāt-ī erant.

1. The wall and the gate were built by Gaius, our friend.
2. The boy and the girl had been taught by the son of the judge.
3. We have seen Julia, your sister, and Lentulus, our friend.
4. The books and the letters were praised by the wise king.
5. Heavy stones had been moved by the great river.
6. We shall have been seen by the Gauls, our enemies.
7. You were frightened by the words of the messengers.
8. The bold slaves had broken the gates of the city.
9. Rome, our city, will be attacked by all the soldiers.
10. The sweet song of the girls will be praised by the queen.
11. We shall be wounded by the heavy spears of the enemy (*pl.*).
12. We were fearing the deep river and the vast sea.

FOURTH DECLENSION

Nouns whose Genitive Singular ends in **ūs** belong to the Fourth Declension.

The Nominative ends in **us** if the Noun is Masculine (or Feminine).

The Nominative ends in **ū** if the Noun is Neuter.

MASCULINE

	SINGULAR		PLURAL	
Nom.	Grad-us	a step (m.)	Grad-ūs	steps
Voc.	Grad-us	O step	Grad-ūs	O steps
Acc.	Grad-um	a step	Grad-ūs	steps
Gen.	Grad-ūs	of a step	Grad-uum	of steps
Dat.	Grad-uī	to or for a step	Grad-ibus	to or for steps
Abl.	Grad-ū	by, with, or from a step	Grad-ibus	by, with, or from steps

NEUTER

	SINGULAR		PLURAL	
Nom.	Gen-ū	a knee (n.)	Gen-ua	knees
Voc.	Gen-ū	O knee	Gen-ua	O knees
Acc.	Gen-ū	a knee	Gen-ua	knees
Gen.	Gen-ūs	of a knee	Gen-uum	of knees
Dat.	Gen-ū	to or for a knee	Gen-ibus	to or for knees
Abl.	Gen-ū	by, with, or from a knee	Gen-ibus	by, with, or from knees

Carefully distinguish the Fourth from the Second Declension—

A Noun with Nominative in **-us** and Genitive in **-ī** is of the Second Declension;

A Noun with Nominative in **-us** and Genitive in **-ūs** is of the Fourth Declension.

RULE.—**When an Adjective describes ' man ' ' woman,' or ' thing,' the Noun is sometimes omitted in Latin, and the Adjective shows by its Gender whether ' man,' ' woman,' or ' thing,' is meant.** Thus—

	SINGULAR		PLURAL	
Masculine,	Bonus	= a good man	Boni	= good men
Feminine,	Bona	= a good woman	Bonae	= good women
Neuter,	Bonum	= a good thing	Bona	= good things

VOCABULARY

Decline—
Like **Gradus**

Arc-us,[1] -ūs, m., *a bow*
Exercit-us, -ūs, m., *an army*
Curr-us, -ūs, m., *a chariot*
Man-us, -ūs, f., *a hand*

Imperāt-or, -ōris, m., *a general*
Rot-a, -ae, f., *a wheel*

EXERCISE XXVII

1. Mīlitēs nostrī arcūs magnōs manibus tenē-bant.
2. Manus tenera sorōris tuae vulnerāt-a erat.
3. Currūs hostium ab omnibus mīlitibus vīs-ī erunt.
4. Omnēs bonī Rōmulum, rēgem nostrum, amā-bunt.
5. Fīlius amīcī tuī ā multīs culpāt-us erat.
6. Exercitūs Gallōrum, hostium nostrōrum, vīd-imus.
7. Fortium opera et sapientium verba laudā-tis.
8. Multī sagittās et arcūs magnōs portāv-ērunt.
9. Caesar, imperātor exercitūs nostrī, hostem non time-t.
10. Puerōrum audācium sagittās manū meā frēg-eram.
11. Magnum exercitum et multōs currūs mīs-istis.
12. Fortēs et sapientēs ab omnibus laudā-buntur.

1. The vast armies of the Gauls were seen by our (men).
2. All your works have been praised by the wise (men).
3. The friends of Gaius, the wise judge, wrote many (things).
4. We shall shut the gates of the city with our (own) hands.
5. You did not see the bows and the arrows of the enemy (*pl.*)
6. Many will blame Caesar, the general of your army.
7. The brave do not fear the armies and chariots of kings.
8. Rome, the city of brave (men), will be attacked by the Gauls.
9. The heavy burden was moved by the hand of a girl.
10. The king and the queen were loved by all good (men).
11. The great stones will break the wheels of the chariots.
12. The rivers hindered the armies of the brave Gauls.

---

[1] Dat. and Abl. Pl. **arc-ubus.**

THIRD CONJUGATION: CONSONANT VERBS
Example—**Reg-ere,** *to rule*
Pres. Stem, **reg-**   *Perf. Stem,* **rēx-**   *Sup. Stem,* **rēct-**

PASSIVE VOICE
TENSES FORMED FROM THE PRESENT STEM **Reg-**

		PRESENT	
	FORMATION	EXAMPLE	ENGLISH
	Present Stem		
Sing. 1	+or	reg-or	*I am (being) ruled*
2	+eris	reg-eris	*You are ruled*
3	+itur	reg-itur	*He is ruled*
Plur. 1	+imur	reg-imur	*We are ruled*
2	+iminī	reg-iminī	*You are ruled*
3	+untur	reg-untur	*They are ruled*

		IMPERFECT	
	Present Stem		
Sing. 1	+ēbar	reg-ēbar	*I was being ruled*
2	+ēbāris	reg-ēbāris [1]	*You were being ruled*
3	+ēbātur	reg-ēbātur	*He was being ruled*
Plur. 1	+ēbāmur	reg-ēbāmur	*We were being ruled*
2	+ēbāminī	reg-ēbāminī	*You were being ruled*
3	+ēbantur	reg-ēbantur	*They were being ruled*

		FUTURE SIMPLE	
	Present Stem		
Sing. 1	+ar	reg-ar	*I shall be ruled*
2	+ēris	reg-ēris [2]	*You will be ruled*
3	+ētur	reg-ētur	*He will be ruled*
Plur. 1	+ēmur	reg-ēmur	*We shall be ruled*
2	+ēminī	reg-ēminī	*You will be ruled*
3	+entur	reg-entur	*They will be ruled*

[1] *or* reg-ēbāre.   [2] *or* reg-ēre.

RULE.—' With,' when it means ' together with,' or ' in company with,' is translated by ' cum,' followed by the Ablative; as, **Servum cum puerō mittō** = *I send the slave with the boy.*

Carefully distinguish this from the Ablative of Instrument, which shows *with* what or *by* what an action is done. See page 54.

Puer sagittīs vulnerātus est = *The boy was wounded with arrows.*

VOCABULARY

Occid-ō (3), *I kill* *Perfect Stem,* **occid-** *Supine Stem,* **occis-**
Gerō- (3), *I carry on* „ **gess-** „ **gest-**
Flūct-us, -ūs, m., *a wave*
Vent-us, -ī, m., *wind*

N.B.—**reg-eris** (short e) is Second Person Singular Present;
   reg-ēris (long e) is Second Person Singular Future.

EXERCISE XXVIII

1. Ā Gallīs vinc-ēmur.
2. Cum nūntiō mitt-eris.
3. Nōn dūc-ēbāminī.
4. Tēlīs occīd-ēris.
5. Cum multīs mitt-ēmur.
6. Bella ger-ēbantur.
7. Ā Caesare dūc-ēbāmur.
8. Omnēs vinc-entur.
9. Multa sapientia ā Lentulō, amīcō tuō, scrīb-untur.
10. Imperātōrem cum omnibus amīcīs occīd-ēmus.
11. Multae nāvēs flūctibus et ventō frang-untur.
12. Mūrum ingentem lapidibus magnīs aedificā-bāmus.
13. Fīliī nostrī cum nūntiīs vēlōcibus mitt-entur.
14. Multī fortēs ā Gallīs, hostibus nostrīs, occīd-ēbantur.
15. Virginis pulchrae carmina dulcia audīv-imus.
16. Librī magnī a Gaiō, iūdice sapientī, scrīb-untur.

1. Vast armies were being led by the brave general.
2. You will be slain by the heavy spear of the Gaul.
3. Many gifts will be sent by Julia, your sister.
4. We shall send a swift messenger with your slave.
5. Our king with (his) son will be slain by the enemy.
6. The gate of the city is being broken with a vast stone.
7. The Gauls with a vast army will attack our city.
8. Brave (men) are not frightened by waves and wind.
9. The wheels of our chariots will be broken by the stones.
10. We shall be led by Caesar, a brave general.
11. Your work has been praised by all good men.
12. The wise praise the good laws of Romulus, our king.

Third Conjugation : Consonant Verbs—*continued*

Example—**Reg-ere,** *to rule*

Pres. Stem, reg-   *Perf. Stem,* rēx-   *Sup. Stem,* rēct-

PASSIVE VOICE

TENSES FORMED FROM THE SUPINE STEM **Rēct-**

			PERFECT AND AORIST	
	FORMATION	EXAMPLE	ENGLISH	
			Perfect	Aorist
	Supine Stem			
Sing. 1	+us sum	rēct-us sum	*I have been*	*I was*
2	+us es	rēct-us es	*You have been*	*You were*
3	+us est	rēct-us est	*He has been*	*He was*
Plur. 1	+ ī sumus	rēct-ī sumus	*We have been*	*We were*
2	+ ī estis	rēct-ī estis	*You have been*	*You were*
3	+ ī sunt	rēct-ī sunt	*They have been*	*They were*

(brace *ruled* for Perfect column; brace *ruled* for Aorist column)

		PLUPERFECT	
	Supine Stem		
Sing. 1	+us eram	rēct-us eram	*I had been ruled*
2	+us erās	rēct-us erās	*You had been ruled*
3	+us erat	rēct-us erat	*He had been ruled*
Plur. 1	+ī erāmus	rēct-ī erāmus	*We had been ruled*
2	+ī erātis	rēct-ī erātis	*You had been ruled*
3	+ī erant	rēct-ī erant	*They had been ruled*

		FUTURE PERFECT	
	Supine Stem		
Sing. 1	+us erō	rēct-us erō	*I shall have been ruled*
2	+us eris	rēct-us eris	*You will have been ruled*
3	+us erit	rēct-us erit	*He will have been ruled*
Plur. 1	+ī erimus	rēct-ī erimus	*We shall have been ruled*
2	+ī eritis	rēct-ī eritis	*You will have been ruled*
3	+ī erunt	rēct-ī erunt	*They will have been ruled*

' To '

The meaning of the Dative is generally indicated in English by ' to ' or ' for ': thus, **Rēgī** = *to* (or *for*) *the king*: but where motion towards is implied, ' to ' is translated by **ad** with the Accusative; as, **Ad urbem missus est** = *he was sent to the city.*

RULE.—' To,' without motion towards—Dative only.

' To,' with motion towards—' ad ' with Accus.

EXERCISE XXIX

[In this and the following Exercises words introduced for the first time are given only in the Vocabulary at the end.]

1. Rēx Gallōrum cum exercitū ad urbem contend-it.
2. Multae nāvēs flūctibus et ventō frāct-ae erant.
3. Nūntiī vēlōcēs ad exercitum nostrum mīss-ī sunt.
4. Urbis portae ā servīs timidīs claus-ae erunt.
5. Hastae et sagittae fuērunt ūtilēs mīlitibus.
6. Librōs Lentulī, amīcī tuī, rēgī mōnstrāv-imus.
7. Rēx et rēgīna omnibus bonīs cārī fu-ērunt.
8. Carmina avium parvārum sunt dulcia omnibus.
9. Urbis turrēs et portās imperātōrī mōnstrā-bimus.
10. Cum multīs Gallīs ad urbem vestram duct-ī sumus.
11. Epistulae brevēs ā sapientibus scrīb-ēbantur.
12. Liber tuus Lentulō, iūdicis fīliō, ūtilis erit.

1. The name of our general is dear to all the soldiers.
2. All the slaves have been sent to the great city.
3. The wall of the temple was broken by the waves.
4. Our armies had been conquered by the Gauls, our enemies.
5. The words of the judges will be declared to the king.
6. The messengers had been sent to the city of the queen.
7. We were marching with a great army to the river.
8. Many brave men were slain by the darts of the enemy.
9. The ships of the enemy were useful to our queen.
10. The wheels of the chariot had been broken by the stones.
11. You will not be blamed by Gaius, a wise master.
12. The letters and books were shown to all the boys.

FIFTH DECLENSION

Nouns whose Genitive Singular ends in **ēī** are of the Fifth Declension. The Nominative Singular ends in **ēs,** and the Gender is Feminine (except **diēs,** usually masc.).

	SINGULAR		PLURAL	
Nom.	Di-ēs	a day (m., f.)	Di-ēs	days
Voc.	Di-ēs	O day	Di-ēs	O days
Acc.	Di-em	a day	Di-ēs	days
Gen.	Di-ēī	of a day	Di-ērum	of days
Dat.	Di-ēī	to or for a day	Di-ēbus	to or for days
Abl.	Di-ē	by, with, or from a day	Di-ēbus	by, with, or from days

CASE-ENDINGS OF THE FIVE DECLENSIONS

	1	2		3		4		5
	Fem.	Masc. Fem.	Neut.	Masc. Fem.	Neut.	Masc. Fem.	Neut.	Fem.
Nom.	-a	-us -er	-um	various	various	-us	-ū	-ēs
Voc.	-a	-e -er	-um	= Nom.	= Nom.	-us	-ū	-ēs
Acc.	-am	-um	-um	-em	= Nom.	-um	-ū	-em
Gen.	-ae	-ī	-ī	-is	-is	-ūs	-ūs	-ēī
Dat.	-ae	-ō	-ō	-ī	-ī	-uī	-ū	-ēī
Abl.	-ā	-ō	-ō	-e	-e	-ū	-ū	-ē
Nom.	-ae	-ī	-a	-ēs	-a	-ūs	-ūa	-ēs
Voc.	-ae	-ī	-a	-ēs	-a	-ūs	-ūa	-ēs
Acc.	-ās	-ōs	-a	-ēs	-a	-ūs	-ūa	-ēs
Gen.	-ārum	-ōrum	-ōrum	{-um -ium}	{-um -ium}	-uum	-uum	-ērum
Dat.	-īs	-īs	-īs	-ibus	-ibus	-ibus	-ibus	ē-bus
Abl.	-īs	-īs	-īs	-ibus	-ibus	-ibus	-ibus	ē-bus

'IN,' 'ON' and 'INTO,' 'ON TO'

The Latin word **in** has two meanings—

In with Accus. means 'into' or 'on to,' and shows motion towards a place;

In with Abl. means 'in,' or 'on,' and shows position in a place.

Thus, **In urbem** = *into the city*; **in urbe** = *in the city*; **in mēnsam** = *on to the table*; **in mēnsā** = *on the table*.

EXERCISE XXX

1. Caesar cum exercitū magnō in Ītaliam contend-ēbat.
2. Rēx et rēgīna in urbe nostrā occīsī erant.
3. Currūs nostrōs et nāvēs amīcō tuō mōnstrā-bāmus.
4. Iūlia, soror tua, ab omnibus bonīs laudāt-a erit.
5. Captīvī miserī ab imperātōre in urbem duct-ī sunt.
6. Cum Lentulō, iūdicis fīliō, in Ītaliam mitt-ēris.
7. Multī mīlitēs sagittīs et hastīs vulnerāt-ī erant.
8. Ītalia, patria nostra, omnibus fortibus cāra est.
9. Servus niger in currū cum imperātōre sedē-bat.
10. Multōs nūntiōs ad iūdicem bonum mīs-istis.
11. Mīlitēs fortēs ā Gallīs, hostibus nostrīs, nōn vinc-entur.
12. Dulcia sunt omnibus sapientibus puellārum carmina.

1. We have not seen Lentulus, the friend of your son.
2. We shall march with Caesar, our general, into Italy.
3. All things will be declared to the judge by the slaves.
4. Many were slain in the town by the arrows of the Gauls.
5. Julia, your sister, is dear to all (her) friends.
6. The slaves were carrying a heavy burden into the town.
7. The armies of our enemies will march into Italy.
8. We were showing our books to Lentulus, your son.
9. Caesar, our general, has carried on many wars.
10. The queen will sit with the king in a beautiful chariot.
11. The words of the general were declared to all the soldiers.
12. Many fishes had been seen in the great river.

F

FOURTH CONJUGATION : Ĭ-VERBS

Audī-re, *to hear*

Pres. Stem, **audī-**　　*Perf. Stem,* **audīv-**　　*Sup. Stem,* **audīt-**

PASSIVE VOICE
TENSES FORMED FROM THE PRESENT STEM **Audī-**

		FORMATION	EXAMPLE	ENGLISH
PRESENT				
		Present Stem		
Sing.	1	+**or**	**audi-or**	*I am (being) heard*
	2	+**ris**	**audī-ris**	*You are heard*
	3	+**tur**	**audī-tur**	*He is heard*
Plur.	1	+**mur**	**audī-mur**	*We are heard*
	2	+**minī**	**audī-minī**	*You are heard*
	3	+**untur**	**audi-untur**	*They are heard*
IMPERFECT				
		Present Stem		
Sing.	1	+**ēbār**	**audi-ēbar**	*I was being heard*
	2	+**ēbāris**	**audi-ēbāris**[1]	*You were being heard*
	3	+**ēbātur**	**audi-ēbātur**	*He was being heard*
Plur.	1	+**ēbāmur**	**audi-ēbāmur**	*We were being heard*
	2	+**ēbāminī**	**audi-ēbāminī**	*You were being heard*
	3	+**ēbantur**	**audi-ēbantur**	*They were being heard*
FUTURE SIMPLE				
		Present Stem		
Sing.	1	+**ar**	**audi-ar**	*I shall be heard*
	2	+**ēris**	**audi-ēris**[2]	*You will be heard*
	3	+**ētur**	**audi-ētur**	*He will be heard*
Plur.	1	+**ēmur**	**audi-ēmur**	*We shall be heard*
	2	+**ēminī**	**audi-ēminī**	*You will be heard*
	3	+**entur**	**audi-entur**	*They will be heard*

RULE.—Time ' when ' is expressed by the Ablative.
　　　　Time ' for how long ' is expressed by the Accusative.

Primō annō occisus est = *he was killed in the first year* (when).
Multōs annōs manēbit = *he will remain many years* (for how long).

---

[1] *or* **audi-ēbāre**.　　　[2] *or* **audi-ēre**.

EXERCISE XXXI

The Latin word **ē** or **ex** means 'from' or 'out of,' and takes an Ablative; as **Ex Ītaliā** = *out of Italy*.

1. Proximō annō omnēs urbēs ā mīlitibus mūni-ēbantur.
2. Ā Lentulō, iūdice sapientī, audi-ērīs.
3. Nāvēs nostrae flūctibus et ventō impedi-untur.
4. Captīvī multōs diēs in oppidō manē-bunt.
5. Prīmō diē nūntiōs ex urbe mīs-imus.
6. Verba tua rēgī et rēgīnae nūntiā-buntur.
7. Puerī ignāvī multās hōrās dormi-ent.
8. Gallī cum exercitū magnō ad urbem contend-ent.
9. Multōs librōs et epistulās manū meā scrīps-ī.
10. Hastae et sagittae mīlitī fortī ūtilēs erunt.
11. Gallōrum imperātor annō secundō occīs-us erat.
12. Carmen puellārum ab omnibus laudāt-um erit.

1. We were being instructed by Lentulus, a wise master.
2. You will be hindered by the river and by the walls.
3. The city is being fortified by Caesar, the general.
4. The next day the slaves were sent out of the town.
5. Many captives were being led into Italy by our (men).
6. The son of the general was wounded with a short spear.
7. We have been sent with the swift messenger to the king.
8. The words of the wise are praised by all good (men).
9. We do not fear the armies of the Gauls, our enemies.
10. The voice of the general will be heard by all the soldiers.
11. The gates of the city will be guarded by a brave (man).
12. The sick (men) slept in (their) beds for many days.

Fourth Conjugation : I-Verbs—*continued*

Example—**Audī-re,** *to hear*

Pres. Stem, **audī-**   *Perf. Stem,* **audīv-**   *Sup. Stem,* **audīt-**

PASSIVE VOICE

TENSES FORMED FROM THE SUPINE STEM **Audīt-**

The Supine Stem of a Regular Verb of the Fourth Conjugation is found by adding **t** to the Present Stem.

PERFECT AND AORIST

	FORMATION	EXAMPLE	ENGLISH	
			Perfect	Aorist
	Supine Stem			
Sing. 1	+**us sum**	audīt-us sum	*I have been*	*I was*
2	+**us es**	audīt-us es	*You have been*	*You were*
3	+**us est**	audīt-us est	*He has been*	*He was*
Plur. 1	+**ī sumus**	audīt-ī sūmus	*We have been*	*We were*
2	+**ī estis**	audīt-ī estis	*You have been*	*You were*
3	+**ī sunt**	audīt-ī sunt	*They have been*	*They were*

(*heard* bracketing Perfect column; *heard* bracketing Aorist column)

PLUPERFECT

	Supine Stem		
Sing. 1	+**us eram**	audīt-us eram	*I had been heard*
2	+**us erās**	audīt-us erās	*You had been heard*
3	+**us erat**	audīt-us erat	*He had been heard*
Plur. 1	+**ī erāmus**	audīt-ī erāmus	*We had been heard*
2	+**ī erātis**	audīt-ī erātis	*You had been heard*
3	+**ī erant**	audīt-ī erant	*They had been heard*

FUTURE PERFECT

	Supine Stem		
Sing. 1	+**us erō**	audīt-us erō	*I shall have been heard*
2	+**us eris**	audīt-us eris	*You will have been heard*
3	+**us erit**	audīt-us erit	*He will have been heard*
Plur. 1	+**ī erimus**	audīt-ī erimus	*We shall have been heard*
2	+**ī eritis**	audīt-ī eritis	*You will have been heard*
3	+**ī erunt**	audīt-ī erunt	*They will have been heard*

A Sentence containing an Active Transitive Verb with an Object can be turned into a Sentence containing a Passive Verb with an Ablative of Agent (or Instrument) or *vice versa*. See page 77.

EXERCISE XXXII

1. Proximō diē omnēs nāvēs nostrae flūctibus frāct-ae sunt.
2. Onus magnum et grave multās hōrās portā-bāmus.
3. Urbis portae ab imperātōre prīmā hōrā claud-entur.
4. Iūdicum fīliī cum nostrīs fīliīs ērudīt-ī sunt.
5. Multōs diēs in Ītaliā cum amīcīs māns-imus.
6. Secundā hōrā nūntium vēlōcem ex urbe mitt-ēmus.
7. Proximō annō exercitum magnum in Ītaliam dūx-ī.
8. Vōcēs puellārum in templīs vestrīs audīt-ae erunt.
9. Multōs diēs in nāve cum mīlitibus manē-bis.
10. Annō secundō Gallī omnēs ā nostrīs vict-ī sunt.
11. Cāra est cīvibus omnibus Ītalia, patria nostra.
12. Exercitūs nostrī ab imperātōre fortī dūc-ēbantur.

1. On the next day a voice was heard in the temples.
2. For many days the captives remained in the city.
3. All the cities of Italy had been fortified by our men.
4. The messenger was sent out of the city at the first hour.
5. The next year many brave (men) were slain by the enemies.
6. The great rivers will hinder the armies of the Gauls.
7. On the second day the town will be attacked by the king.
8. The messengers had declared your words to the judge.
9. You were seen by Gaius, our slave, and by many citizens.
10. We feared the darts of the enemy and the waves of the sea.
11. For many hours we sat with the captives in the temple.
12. At the first hour the ships were seen by our messengers.

TABLE OF THE FOUR CONJUGATIONS

PASSIVE VOICE. For Table of Active Voice, see p. 40

		SINGULAR			PLURAL		
		1	2	3	1	2	3
Present	Amā-	or [1]	ris	tur	mur	minī	ntur
	Monē-	or	ris	tur	mur	minī	ntur
	Reg-	or	eris	itur	imur	iminī	untur
	Audī-	or	ris	tur	mur	minī	untur
Imperfect	Amā- Monē- Reg- Audī-	bar ēbar	bāris ēbāris	bātur ēbātur	bāmur ēbāmur	bāminī ēbāminī	bantur ēbantur
Future Simple	Amā- Monē- Reg- Audī	bor ar	beris ēris	bitur ētur	bimur ēmur	biminī ēminī	buntur entur
Perfect & Aorist	Amāt- Monit- Rēct- Audīt-	us sum	us es	us est	ī sumus	ī estis	ī sunt
Pluperfect	Amāt- Monit- Rēct- Audīt-	us eram	us erās	us erat	ī erāmus	ī erātis	ī erant
Future Perfect	Amāt- Monit- Rēct- Audīt-	us erō	us eris	us erit	ī erimus	ī eritis	ī erunt

ENGLISH

Present—*I am being loved, or am loved, etc.*
Imperfect—*I was being loved, etc.*
Future Simple—*I shall be loved, etc.*
{ Perfect—*I have been loved, etc.*
{ Aorist—*I was loved, etc.*
Pluperfect—*I had been loved, etc.*
Future Perfect—*I shall have been loved, etc.*

---

[1] The First Person Singular Present is **amor** for **amāor**.

RECAPITULATORY

Active and Passive Voices, Four Conjugations

1. Vidē-bar.	10. Vocāt-a erit.	19. Sci-et.
2. Culpā-beris.	11. Sedē-bās.	20. Manē-bunt.
3. Dūc-ēris.	12. Mūni-ēmus.	21. Dūc-iminī.
4. Sci-unt.	13. Custōdī-tis.	22. Habē-tis.
5. Vinc-ētur.	14. Vocā-bimur.	23. Vinc-ēbāris.
6. Terrē-tur.	15. Doct-ī erant.	24. Mōnstrāv-istī.
7. Movē-mur.	16. Terrē-ris.	25. Vocāt-us es.
8. Mōnstrā-ntur.	17. Aedificā-tis.	26. Vītā-minī.
9. Vinc-ar.	18. Miss-a est.	27. Movē-ris.

1. We are conquering.	9. You (s.) will be blamed.
2. You (pl.) were seen.	10. We are instructed.
3. She has been taught.	11. He is being praised.
4. We are being led.	12. They are building.
5. You (s.) will write.	13. They did not fear.
6. We shall be sent.	14. You (pl.) are not seen.
7. They were avoided.	15. She had been sent.
8. I was being called.	16. I shall have written.

FORMULA FOR INVERSION OF SENTENCES

The Subject of the Active Sentence becomes the Ablative of Agent (or Instrument) in the Passive Sentence. The Object of the Active Sentence becomes the Subject of the Passive Sentence.

S.   O.   V.T.
Magister puerum laudat.

S.   AB. A.   V.P.
Puer ā magistrō laudātur.

It will be found useful to practise this inversion by turning sentences from Active to Passive and from Passive to Active in any Exercise from No. VIII.

COMPARISON OF ADJECTIVES

Adjectives have three degrees of Comparison, viz.:—

Positive	Comparative	Superlative
Dūr-us, *hard*	**dūr-ior,** *harder*	**dūr-issimus,** { *hardest* / *very hard* }

RULE FOR FORMING DEGREES OF COMPARISON

The Comparative is formed from the Positive by adding **-ior** to what remains after the ending of the Genitive Singular has been removed.

Thus:—**dūrus,** Gen. s.m. **dūr-ī,** Comparative **dūr-ior.**

The Superlative is formed from the Positive in the same way by adding **-issimus.**

Thus:—**dūrus,** Gen. s.m. **dūr-ī,** Superlative **dūr-issimus.**

DECLENSION OF COMPARATIVE AND SUPERLATIVE DEGREES

All Comparatives are declined like **melior, melius,** p. 56.
All Superlatives   ,,   ,,   **bonus, bona, bonum.**

EXAMPLES

Positive	Comparative	Superlative
Cār-us, *dear*	**cār-ior, -ius**	**cār-issimus, -a, -um**
Long-us, *long*	**long-ior, -ius**	**long-issimus, -a, -um**
Trīst-is, *sad*	**trīst-ior, -ius**	**trīst-issimus, -a, -um**
Dulc-is, *sweet*	**dulc-ior, -ius**	**dulc-issimus, -a, -um**
Fēlīx, *happy*	**fēlīc-ior, -ius**	**fēlīc-issimus, -a, -um**
Ingēns, *vast*	**ingēnt-ior, -ius**	**ingēnt-issimus, -a, -um**

RULE.—**Two Nouns joined by ' quam ' (than) must be in the same Case;** thus, **Servus fēlīcior est quam rēx** = *the slave is happier than the king.* Here both *slave* and *king* are in the Nominative.

EXERCISE XXXIII

1. Amīcus meus est omnium iūdicum sapientissimus.
2. Sagittae nostrae breviōrēs sunt quam hasta tua.
3. Proximō diē nūntium vēlōcissimum ex urbe mīs-ī.
4. Carmina dulcissima puellārum nōn audīv-istis.
5. Servī miserī onus gravissimum portāv-erant.
6. Fortissimī mīlitum nostrōrum ā Gallīs occīs-ī erant.
7. Lentulī, iūdicis sapientissimī, verba laudā-bāmus.
8. Templum Diānae altius est quam mūrus noster.
9. Multōs annōs in urbe iūcundissimā māns-imus.
10. Nostrī librī ūtiliōrēs sunt quam vestrī (librī).
11. Gaium occīdistī, omnium cīvium fortissimum.
12. Imperātōrem āudāciōrem quam Caesarem nōn vīdī.

1. A sweeter song.	7. By a very bold man.
2. The heaviest burden.	8. By a heavier stone.
3. Very brave (men).	9. With dearest friends.
4. More beautiful girls.	10. Sweeter songs.
5. Of a shorter letter.	11. A wiser word.
6. Of longer spears.	12. Of heavier darts.

13. The spears of the Gauls are longer than ours (*i.e.* our spears).
14. We shall send Gaius, the boldest of all the citizens.
15. The songs of little birds are sweeter than your voice.
16. I hear the voice of Lentulus, a very brave soldier.
17. To a wise man books are more useful than spears.
18. We have not seen a more pleasant land than Italy.

COMPARISON OF ADJECTIVES

ADJECTIVES ENDING IN **-er**

Adjectives in **-er** (like **niger** and **tener**) form their Comparative according to the rule already given (p. 78), but their Superlative is formed by adding **-rimus** to the Masculine Nominative Singular.

Positive	Comparative	Superlative
Niger, *black*	**nigr-ior, -ius**	**niger-rimus, -a, -um**
Tener, *tender*	**tener-ior, -ius**	**tener-rimus, -a, -um**
Pulcher, *beautiful*	**pulchr-ior, -ius**	**pulcher-rimus, -a, -um**

SIX ADJECTIVES FORM SUPERLATIVE IN **-limus**

Positive	Comparative	Superlative
Facil-is, *easy*	**facil-ior, -ius**	**facil-limus, -a, -um**
Difficil-is, *difficult*	**difficil-ior, -ius**	**difficil-limus, -a, -um**
Simil-is, *like*	**simil-ior, -ius**	**simil-limus, -a, -um**
Dissimil-is, *unlike*	**dissimil-ior, -ius**	**dissimil-limus, -a, -um**
Gracil-is, *slender*	**gracil-ior, -ius**	**gracil-limus, -a, -um**
Humil-is, *low*	**humil-ior, -ius**	**humil-limus, -a, -um**

IRREGULAR

Positive	Comparative	Superlative
Bonus, *good*	**meli-or, -us**	**optimus, -a, -um**
Malus, *bad*	**pei-or, -us**	**pessimus, -a, -um**
Magnus, *great*	**mai-or, -us**	**maximus, -a, -um**
Parvus, *small*	**min-or, -us**	**minimus, -a, -um**
Multus, $\begin{Bmatrix} much \\ many \end{Bmatrix}$	**plūs** (neut.)	**plūrimus, -a, -um**

EXERCISE XXXIV

1. Patrēs nostrī urbem pulcherrimam aedificāv-ērunt.
2. Optimum dōnum ā Lentulō, amīcō meō, miss-um est.
3. Virginēs pulcherrimae carmen melius cantā-bant.
4. Rōma, urbs maxima, ā Gallīs oppugnāt-a erit.
5. Nāvēs minōrēs flūctibus et ventō frang-entur.
6. Gaium, cīvem pessimum, ex Ītaliā mīs-erāmus.
7. Verba iūdicis optimī ab omnibus laudā-buntur.
8. Imperātōris fīlius est omnium puerōrum minimus.
9. Verba amīcī tuī peiōra fu-ērunt quam facta.
10. Servī miserrimī opus difficillimum timē-bant.
11. Maxima opera mīlitibus nostrīs sunt facillima.
12. Plūrimī captīvī ab hostibus nostrīs occīd-ēbantur.

1. We have seen Rome, the largest city of Italy.
2. Very many brave (men) were slain by the Gauls.
3. We shall show the best books to Julia, your sister.
4. Caesar, with a very large army, is marching into Italy.
5. The boldest soldiers feared the chariots of the enemy.
6. You have never seen a larger river than the Rhine.
7. The books were written by Gaius, a very bad judge.
8. A very great forest will hinder Caesar's army.
9. The best citizens are praised by Romulus, the king.
10. The deeds of many (men) are better than (their) words.
11. We shall remain many days in a very beautiful city.
12. The worst boys will be sent to (their) beds.

EXERCISE XXXV

1. Multa dōna ā Iūliā, sorōre tuā, mitt-entur.
2. Rēx noster cum fīliō suō ab hostibus occīs-us est.
3. Urbis portae lapide ingentī frang-ēbantur.
4. Nūntiī vēlōcēs in urbem rēgīnae mīss-ī erant.
5. Hostium nāvēs imperātōrī nostrō ūtilēs erunt.
6. Ā Gaiō, magistrō sapientissimō, nōn culpā-beris.
7. Lentulō, amīcō tuō, librōs nostrōs mōnstrā-bimus.
8. Imperātōris verba mīlitibus omnibus nūntia-ntur.
9. Puellam pulchriōrem quam Iūliam nōn vīdimus.
10. Proximō annō multī ā Gallīs occīs-ī sunt.
11. Multōs diēs in Ītaliā cum Lentulō māns-imus.
12. Exercitūs nostrī silvīs maximīs impedīt-ī sunt.
13. Fēminīs hastae nōn sunt in bellō ūtilissimae.
14. Plūrimōs piscēs in flūminibus nostrīs habē-mus.
15. Quis fēminam in templō vīd-it?

1. Our walls are higher than the temple of Diana.
2. On the next day many very brave (men) were slain.
3. The words of the wise are praised by all good (men).
4. The gates of the city were shut at the second hour.
5. The Gauls, our enemies, were marching into Italy.
6. We shall announce your words to Caesar, the general.
7. All the books were written by a very wise (man).
8. We shall march with your soldiers into Italy.
9. The boys and the girls will have been praised by all.
10. The king and the queen are dear to all the citizens.
11. Many ships will be sent by the brave general.
12. You have heard the very sweet song of the girls.
13. All the Gauls know the causes of the war.
14. Swords are not feared by the bravest soldiers.
15. Few (men) have a bed longer than my (bed).

EXERCISE XXXVI

1. Rōma, urbs pulcherrima, ā Gallīs oppugnāt-a erat.
2. Dulcis est vōx tua: dulcius est avium carmen.
3. Hostium nāvēs maiōrēs erant quam nostrae (nāvēs).
4. Optimī mīlitēs ab imperātōre fortī laudā-bantur.
5. Gaius, amīcus tuus, plūrimōs librōs scrīps-it.
6. Lentulī fīlius omnium iūdicum est sapientissimus.
7. Servōs et cīvēs pessimōs ex urbe mīs-erāmus.
8. Plūrimās hastās et sagittās manibus frēg-imus.
9. Urbēs omnēs ab imperātōribus nostrīs mūni-untur.
10. Servī miserī onus gravissimum portā-bant.
11. Cīvēs omnēs iūdicis sapientis verba lauda-nt.
12. Currūs et nāvēs hostium nōn timē-bimus.
13. Servī Caesaris hastās in agrīs nōn habē-bunt.
14. Mēnsae ā virginibus pulcherrimīs parāt-ae erant.
15. Lupī in silvīs Britanniae nōn vide-ntur.

1. The wall is high: the temple of Diana is higher.
2. We shall send a swifter messenger than your slave.
3. The armies of the Gauls are larger than our (armies).
4. The name of the queen is dear to many brave (men).
5. Your words are wise: your books will be very useful.
6. She was wounded with a heavy spear by the slave.
7. We shall not march with your general into Italy.
8. On the next day we sent a swift messenger to the city.
9. Many captives are being led by Caesar into the town.
10. A slave was sitting in the general's chariot.
11. The judge's sons were blamed by all wise men.
12. The captives will remain in the town for many years.
13. The rivers of Britain have very many fish.
14. Who knows the cause of the danger?
15. The soldier has hidden (his) sword on the island.

Second Steps in Latin, by the same Author, supplies a direct sequel to this book.

Fabulae Faciles, an easy Translation Book, may be used in conjunction with *Second Steps in Latin.*

APPENDIX

NOUNS

FIRST DECLENSION. GEN. SING. -ae

	SINGULAR		PLURAL
Nom.	**Mēns-a**, *a table (f.)*		**Mēns-ae**, *tables*
Voc.	**Mēns-a**, *O table*		**Mēns-ae**, *O tables*
Acc.	**Mēns-am**, *a table*		**Mēns-ās**, *tables*
Gen.	**Mēns-ae**, *of a table*		**Mēns-ārum**, *of tables*
Dat.	**Mēns-ae**, *to or for a table*		**Mēns-īs**, *to or for tables*
Abl.	**Mēns-ā**, *by, with, or from a table*		**Mēns-īs**, *by, with, or from tables*

SECOND DECLENSION. GEN. SING. -ī

(*a*) MASCULINE

	SINGULAR		PLURAL
Nom.	**Domin-us**, *a lord (m.)*	*Nom.*	**Domin-ī**, *lords*
Voc.	**Domin-e**	*Voc.*	**Domin-ī**
Acc.	**Domin-um**	*Acc.*	**Domin-ōs**
Gen.	**Domin-ī**	*Gen.*	**Domin-ōrum**
Dat.	**Domin-ō**	*Dat.*	**Domin-īs**
Abl.	**Domin-ō**	*Abl.*	**Domin-īs**

	SINGULAR		PLURAL
Nom.	**Magister**, *a master (m.)*	*Nom.*	**Magistr-ī**, *masters*
Voc.	**Magister**	*Voc.*	**Magistr-ī**
Acc.	**Magistr-um**	*Acc.*	**Magistr-ōs**
Gen.	**Magistr-ī**	*Gen.*	**Magistr-ōrum**
Dat.	**Magistr-ō**	*Dat.*	**Magistr-īs**
Abl.	**Magistr-ō**	*Abl.*	**Magistr-īs**

	SINGULAR		PLURAL
Nom.	**Puer**, *a boy (m.)*	*Nom.*	**Puer-ī**, *boys*
Voc.	**Puer**	*Voc.*	**Puer-ī**
Acc.	**Puer-um**	*Acc.*	**Puer-ōs**
Gen.	**Puer-ī**	*Gen.*	**Puer-ōrum**
Dat.	**Puer-ō**	*Dat.*	**Puer-īs**
Abl.	**Puer-ō**	*Abl.*	**Puer-īs**

(*b*) NEUTER

	SINGULAR		PLURAL
Nom. Voc. Acc.	**Bell-um**, *war (n.)*	*Nom. Voc. Acc.*	**Bell-a**, *wars*
Gen.	**Bell-ī**	*Gen.*	**Bell-ōrum**
Dat. Abl.	**Bell-ō**	*Dat. Abl.*	**Bell-īs**

THIRD DECLENSION. Gen. Sing. -is

INCREASING NOUNS. Gen. Plur. -um

(a) Masculine and Feminine

SINGULAR		PLURAL	
Nom. Voc.	Iūdex, *judge* (*m.*)	Nom. Voc.	Iūdic-ēs, *judges*
Acc.	Iūdic-em	Acc.	Iūdic-ēs
Gen.	Iūdic-is	Gen.	Iūdic-um
Dat.	Iūdic-ī	Dat.	Iūdic-ibus
Abl.	Iūdic-e	Abl.	Iūdic-ibus

SINGULAR		PLURAL	
Nom. Voc.	Virgō, *maiden* (*f.*)	Nom. Voc.	Virgin-ēs, *maidens*
Acc.	Virgin-em	Acc.	Virgin-ēs
Gen.	Virgin-is	Gen.	Virgin-um
Dat.	Virgin-ī	Dat.	Virgin-ibus
Abl.	Virgin-e	Abl.	Virgin-ibus

(b) Neuter

SINGULAR		PLURAL	
Nom. Voc. Acc.	Nōmen, *name* (*n.*)	Nom. Voc. Acc.	Nōmin-a, *names*
Gen.	Nōmin-is	Gen.	Nōmin-um
Dat.	Nōmin-ī	Dat.	Nōmin-ibus
Abl.	Nōmin-e	Abl.	Nōmin-ibus

SINGULAR		PLURAL	
Nom. Voc. Acc.	Opus, *work* (*n.*)	Nom. Voc. Acc.	Oper-a, *works*
Gen.	Oper-is	Gen.	Oper-um
Dat.	Oper-ī	Dat.	Oper-ibus
Abl.	Oper-e	Abl.	Oper-ibus

NON-INCREASING NOUNS. Gen. Plur. -ium

(a) Masculine and Feminine

SINGULAR		PLURAL	
Nom. Voc.	Ov-is, *sheep* (*f.*)	Nom. Voc.	Ov-ēs, *sheep*
Acc.	Ov-em	Acc.	Ov-ēs
Gen.	Ov-is	Gen.	Ov-ium
Dat.	Ov-ī	Dat.	Ov-ibus
Abl.	Ov-e	Abl.	Ov-ibus

(b) Neuter

SINGULAR		PLURAL	
Nom. Voc. Acc.	Cubīl-e, *bed* (*n.*)	Nom. Voc. Acc.	Cubīl-ia, *beds*
Gen.	Cubīl-is	Gen.	Cubīl-ium
Dat. Abl.	Cubīl-ī	Dat. Abl.	Cubīl-ibus

FOURTH DECLENSION. GEN. SING. -ūs

	SINGULAR		PLURAL
Nom. Voc.	Grad-us, *step (m.)*	*Nom. Voc.*	Grad-ūs, *steps*
Acc.	Grad-um	*Acc.*	Grad-ūs
Gen.	Grad-ūs	*Gen.*	Grad-uum
Dat.	Grad-uī	*Dat.*	Grad-ibus
Abl.	Grad-ū	*Abl.*	Grad-ibus

Nom. Voc. Acc.	Gen-ū, *knee (n.)*	*Nom. Voc. Acc.*	Gen-ua, *knees*
Gen.	Gen-ūs	*Gen.*	Gen-uum
Dat. Abl.	Gen-ū	*Dat. Abl.*	Gen-ibus

FIFTH DECLENSION. GEN. SING. -ēī

	SINGULAR		PLURAL
Nom. Voc.	Di-ēs, *day (m. f.)*	*Nom. Voc.*	Di-ēs, *days*
Acc.	Di-em	*Acc.*	Di-ēs
Gen.	Di-ēī	*Gen.*	Di-ērum
Dat.	Di-ēī	*Dat.*	Di-ēbus
Abl.	Di-ē	*Abl.*	Di-ēbus

ADJECTIVES OF FIRST AND SECOND DECLENSIONS

	SINGULAR			PLURAL		
	Masc.	Fem.	Neut.	Masc.	Fem.	Neut.
Nom.	Bon-us	bon-a	bon-um	Bon-ī	bon-ae	bon-a
Voc.	Bon-e	bon-a	bon-um	Bon-ī	bon-ae	bon-a
Acc.	Bon-um	bon-am	bon-um	Bon-ōs	bon-ās	bon-a
Gen.	Bon-ī	bon-ae	bon-ī	Bon-ōrum	bon-ārum	bon-ōrum
Dat.	Bon-ō	bon-ae	bon-ō	Bon-īs	bon-īs	bon-īs
Abl.	Bon-ō	bon-ā	bon-ō	Bon-īs	bon-īs	bon-īs
Nom.	Niger	nigr-a	nigr-um	Nigr-ī	nigr-ae	nigr-a
Voc.	Niger	nigr-a	nigr-um	Nigr-ī	nigr-ae	nigr-a
Acc.	Nigr-um	nigr-am	nigr-um	Nigr-ōs	nigr-ās	nigr-a
Gen.	Nigr-ī	nigr-ae	nigr-ī	Nigr-ōrum	nigr-ārum	nigr-ōrum
Dat.	Nigr-ō	nigr-ae	nigr-ō	Nigr-is	nigr-is	nigr-is
Abl.	Nigr-ō	nigr-ā	nigr-ō	Nigr-is	nigr-is	nigr-is
Nom.	Tener	tener-a	tener-um	Tener-ī	tener-ae	tener-a
Voc.	Tener	tener-a	tener-um	Tener-ī	tener-ae	tener-a
Acc.	Tener-um	tener-am	tener-um	Tener-ōs	tener-ās	tener-a
Gen.	Tener-ī	tener-ae	tener-ī	Tener-ōrum	tener-ārum	tener-ōrum
Dat.	Tener-ō	tener-ae	tener-ō	Tener-is	tener-is	tener-is
Abl.	Tener-ō	tener-ā	tener-ō	Tener-is	tener-is	tener-is

G

ADJECTIVES OF THIRD DECLENSION

	SINGULAR	
	Masc. or Fem.	Neut.
N. V.	Melior	melius, *better*
Acc.	Meliōr-em	melius
Gen.	Meliōr-is	meliōr-is
Dat.	Meliōr-ī	meliōr-ī
Abl.	Meliōr-e	meliōr-e

	SINGULAR	
	Masc. or Fem.	Neut.
Nom. Vcc.	Trist-is	trīst-e, *sad*
Acc.	Trist-em	trist-e
Gen.	Trist-is	trīst-is
Dat.	Trist-ī	trīst-ī
Abl.	Trist-ī	trīst-ī

	PLURAL	
	Masc. or Fem.	Neut.
N. V. A.	Meliōr-ēs	meliōr-a
Gen.	Meliōr-um	meliōr-um
Dat. Abl.	Meliōr-ibus	meliōr-ibus

	PLURAL	
	Masc. or Fem.	Neut.
N. V. A.	Trīst-ēs	trīst-ia
Gen.	Trīst-ium	trīst-ium
Dat. Abl.	Trīst-ibus	trīst-ibus

	SINGULAR	
	Masc. or Fem.	Neut.
Nom. Voc.	Fēlix, *happy*	fēlix
Acc.	Fēlic-em	fēlix
Gen.	Fēlic-is	fēlic-is
Dat.	Fēlic-ī	fēlic-ī
Abl.	Fēlic-ī	fēlic-ī

	SINGULAR	
	Masc. or Fem.	Neut.
Nom. Voc.	Ingēns, *huge*	ingēns
Acc.	Ingent-em	ingēns
Gen.	Ingent-is	ingent-is
Dat.	Ingent-ī	ingent-ī
Abl.	Ingent-ī	ingent-ī

	PLURAL	
	Masc. or Fem.	Neut.
N. V. A.	Fēlīc-ēs	fēlīc-ia
Gen.	Fēlīc-ium	fēlīc-ium
Dat. Abl.	Fēlīc-ibus	fēlīc-ibus

	PLURAL	
	Masc. or Fem.	Neut.
N. V. A.	Ingent-ēs	ingent-ia
Gen.	Ingent-ium	ingent-ium
Dat. Abl.	Ingent-ibus	ingent-ibus

NUMERALS (up to 20)

1.	I.	ūnus		11.	XI.	ūndecim
2.	II.	duo		12.	XII.	duodecim
3.	III.	trēs		13.	XIII.	tredecim
4.	IV.	quattuor		14.	XIV.	quattuordecim
5.	V.	quīnque		15.	XV.	quīndecim
6.	VI.	sex		16.	XVI.	sēdecim
7.	VII.	septem		17.	XVII.	septendecim
8.	VIII.	octō		18.	XVIII.	duodēvīgintī
9.	IX.	novem		19.	XIX.	ūndēvīgintī
10.	X.	decem		20.	XX.	vīgintī

THE VERB SUM, 'I Am'

PRESENT STEM Es-

	PRESENT	IMPERFECT	FUTURE SIMPLE
	I am	*I was*	*I shall be*
Sing. 1	sum	eram	erō
2	es	erās	eris
3	es-t	erat	erit
Plur. 1	sumus	erāmus	erimus
2	es-tis	erātis	erĭtis
3	sunt	erant	erunt

PERFECT STEM Fu-

	PERFECT AND AORIST	PLUPERFECT	FUTURE PERFECT
	I have been. I was	*I had been*	*I shall have been*
Sing. 1	fu-ī	fu-eram	fu-erō
2	fu-istī	fu-erās	fu-eris
3	fu-it	fu-erat	fu-erit
Plur. 1	fu-imus	fu-erāmus	fu-erimus
2	fu-istis	fu-erātis	fu-eritis
3	fu-ērunt *or* ēre	fu-erant	fu-erint

ACTIVE

Present Stem Tenses

		PRESENT	IMPERFECT	FUTURE SIMPLE
First Conjugation		*I love, am loving, do love*	*I was loving*	*I shall love*
	Sing. 1	amō	amā-bam	amā-bō
	2	amā-s	amā-bās	amā-bis
	3	ama-t	amā-bat	amā-bit
	Plur. 1	amā-mus	amā-bāmus	amā-bimus
	2	amā-tis	amā-bātis	amā-bitis
	3	ama-nt	amā-bant	amā-bunt
Second Conjugation		*I advise, am advising, do advise*	*I was advising*	*I shall advise*
	Sing. 1	monē-ō	monē-bam	monē-bō
	2	monē-s	monē-bās	monē-bis
	3	mone-t	monē-bat	monē-bit
	Plur. 1	monē-mus	monē-bāmus	monē-bimus
	2	monē-tis	monē-bātis	monē-bitis
	3	mone-nt	monē-bant	monē-bunt
Third Conjugation		*I rule, am ruling, do rule*	*I was ruling*	*I shall rule*
	Sing. 1	reg-ō	reg-ēbam	reg-am
	2	reg-is	reg-ēbās	reg-ēs
	3	reg-it	reg-ēbat	reg-et
	Plur. 1	reg-imus	reg-ēbāmus	reg-ēmus
	2	reg-itis	reg-ēbātis	reg-ētis
	3	reg-unt	reg-ēbant	reg-ent
Fourth Conjugation		*I hear, am hearing, do hear*	*I was hearing*	*I shall hear*
	Sing. 1	audī-ō	audi-ēbam	audi-am
	2	audī-s	audi-ēbās	audi-ēs
	3	audī-t	audi-ēbat	audi-et
	Plur. 1	audī-mus	audi-ēbāmus	audi-ēmus
	2	audī-tis	audi-ēbātis	audi-ētis
	3	audi-unt	audi-ēbant	audi-ent

VOICE

Perfect Stem Tenses

	PERFECT AND AORIST	PLUPERFECT	FUTURE PERFECT
	I have loved, *I loved*	*I had loved*	*I shall have loved*
Sing. 1	amāv-ī	amāv-eram	amāv-erō
2	amāv-istī	amāv-erās	amāv-eris
3	amāv-it	amāv-erat	amāv-erit
Plur. 1	amāv-imus	amāv-erāmus	amāv-erimus
2	amāv-istis	amāv-erātis	amāv-eritis
3	amāv-ērunt *or* -ēre	amāv-erānt	amāv-erint
	I have advised, *I advised*	*I had advised*	*I shall have* *advised*
Sing. 1	monu-ī	monu-eram	monu-erō
2	monu-istī	monu-erās	monu-eris
3	monu-it	monu-erat	monu-erit
Plur. 1	monu-imus	monu-erāmus	monu-erimus
2	monu-istis	monu-erātis	monu-eritis
3	monu-ērunt *or* -ēre	monu-erant	monu-erint
	I have ruled, *I ruled*	*I had ruled*	*I shall have ruled*
Sing. 1	rēx-ī	rēx-eram	rēx-erō
2	rēx-istī	rēx-erās	rēx-eris
3	rēx-it	rēx-erat	rēx-erit
Plur. 1	rēximus	rēx-erāmus	rēx-erimus
2	rēx-istis	rēx-erātis	rēx-eritis
3	rēx-ērunt *or* -ēre	rēx-erant	rēx-erint
	I have heard, *I heard*	*I had heard*	*I shall have heard*
Sing. 1	audīv-ī	audīv-eram	audīv-erō
2	audīv-istī	audīv-erās	audīv-eris
3	audīv-it	audīv-erat	audīv-erit
Plur. 1	audīv-imus	audīv-erāmus	audīv-erimus
2	audīv-istis	audīv-erātis	audīv-eritis
3	audīv-ērunt *or* -ēre	audīv-erant	audīv-erint

PASSIVE

Present Stem Tenses

		PRESENT	IMPERFECT	FUTURE SIMPLE
First Conjugation		*I am being loved*	*I was being loved*	*I shall be loved*
	Sing. 1	amo-r	amā-bar	amā-bor
	2	amā-ris	amā-bāris *or* -bāre	amā-beris *or* -bere
	3	amā-tur	amā-bātur	amā-bitur
	Plur. 1	amā-mur	amā-bāmur	amā-bimur
	2	amā-minī	amā-bāminī	amā-biminī
	3	ama-ntur	amā-bantur	amā-buntur
Second Conjugation		*I am being advised*	*I was being advised*	*I shall be advised*
	Sing. 1	mone-or	monē-bar	monē-bor
	2	monē-ris	monē-bāris *or* -bāre	monē-beris *or* -bere
	3	monē-tur	monē-bātur	monē-bitur
	Plur. 1	monē-mur	monē-bāmur	monē-bimur
	2	monē-minī	monē-bāminī	monē-biminī
	3	mone-ntur	monē-bantur	monē-buntur
Third Conjugation		*I am being ruled*	*I was being ruled*	*I shall be ruled*
	Sing. 1	reg-or	reg-ēbar	reg-ar
	2	reg-eris	reg-ēbaris *or* -ēbāre	reg-ēris *or* -ēre
	3	reg-itur	reg-ēbātur	reg-ētur
	Plur. 1	reg-imur	reg-ēbāmur	reg-ēmur
	2	reg-iminī	reg-ēbāminī	reg-ēminī
	3	reg-untur	reg-ēbantur	reg-entur
Fourth Conjugation		*I am being heard*	*I was being heard*	*I shall be heard*
	Sing. 1	audi-or	audi-ēbar	audi-ar
	2	audī-ris	audi-ēbāris *or* -ēbāre	audi-ēris *or* -ēre
	3	audī-tur	audi-ēbātur	audi-ētur
	Plur. 1	audī-mur	audi-ēbāmur	audi-ēmur
	2	audī-minī	audi-ēbāminī	audi-ēminī
	3	audi-untur	audi-ēbantur	audi-entur

VOICE

<small>SUPINE STEM TENSES</small>

	PERFECT AND AORIST	PLUPERFECT	FUTURE PERFECT
	I have been, I was, loved	*I had been loved*	*I shall have been loved*
Sing. 1	amāt-us sum	amāt-us eram	amāt-us erō
2	amāt-us es	amāt-us erās	amāt-us eris
3	amāt-us est	amāt-us crat	amāt-us erit
Plur. 1	amāt-ī sumus	amāt-ī erāmus	amāt-ī erimus
2	amāt-ī estis	amāt-ī erātis	amāt-ī eritis
3	amāt-ī sunt	amāt-ī erant	amāt-ī erunt
	I huve been, I was, advised	*I had been advised*	*I shall have been advised*
Sing. 1	monit-us sum	monit-us eram	monit-us erō
2	monit-us es	monit-us erās	monit-us eris
3	monit-us est	monit-us erat	monit-us erit
Plur. 1	monit-ī sumus	monit-ī erāmus	monit-ī erimus
2	monit-ī estis	monit-ī erātis	monit-ī eritis
3	monit-ī sunt	monit-ī erant	monit-ī erunt
	I have been, I was, ruled	*I had been ruled*	*I shall have been ruled*
Sing. 1	rēct-us sum	rēct-us cram	rēct-us erō
2	rēct-us es	rēct-us erās	rēct-us eris
3	rēct-us est	rēct-us erat	rēct-us erit
Plur. 1	rēct-ī sumus	rēct-ī erāmus	rēct-ī erimus
2	rēct-ī estis	rēct-ī erātis	rēct-ī eritis
3	rēct-ī sunt	rēct-ī erant	rēct-ī erunt
	I have been, I was, heard	*I had been heard*	*I shall have been heard*
Sing. 1	audīt-us sum	audīt-us eram	audīt-us erō
2	audīt-us es	audīt-us erās	audīt-us eris
3	audīt-us est	audīt-us erat	audīt-us erit
Plur. 1	audīt-ī sumus	audit-i erāmus	audīt-ī erimus
2	audīt-ī estis	audīt-ī erātis	audīt-ī eritis
3	audīt-ī sunt	audīt-ī erant	audīt-ī erunt

VOCABULARY

Nouns.—The Nominative Singular, the Genitive Singular, and the Gender are given. The Declension is known from the ending of the Genitive.

Declensions	1	2	3	4	5
Genitives	-ae	-ī	-is	-ūs	-ēī

Adjectives.—Adjectives like *bonus*, *niger*, or *tener* have the three terminations of Nominative Singular given. Other Adjectives are referred to their types.

Verbs.—The Principal Parts of all Latin Verbs are given with a figure enclosed in a bracket to show the Conjugation. The Stem is marked off from the termination by a hyphen, thus:—

PRESENT	PERFECT	SUPINE
mitt-ō	mīs-ī	miss-um

LATIN-ENGLISH

aedific-ō, aedificā-re, aedificāv-ī, aedificāt-um, (1), to build
aeger, aegr-a, aegr-um, *adj.* sick
ager, agrī, *m.*, a field
alt-us, alt-a, alt-um, *adj.* high, deep
amīc-us, -ī, *m.* a friend
ann-us, -ī, *m.* a year
aqu-a, -ae, *f.* water
arc-us, -ūs, *m.* a bow
audāx, audāc-is, *adj.* bold (like fēlīx)
av-is, -is, *f.* a bird

brev-is, brev-e, *adj.* short (like trīstis)
Britanni-a, -ae, *f.*, Britain

Caesar, Caesar-is, *m.* Caesar (a name)
cant-ō, cantā-re, cantāv-ī, cantāt-um (1), to sing

captīv-us, -ī, *m.* a captive
carmen, carmin-is, *n.* a song
cār-us, -a, -um, *adj.* dear
caus-a, -ae, *f.*, a cause
cēl-ō, cēlā-re, celāv-ī, cēlāt-um (1), to hide
cīv-is, -is, *c.* a citizen
claud-ō, claudere, claus-ī, claus-um (3), to shut
contend-ō, contendere, contend-ī, content-um (3), to march
cubīl-e, -is, *n.*, a bed
culp-ō, culpā-re, culpāv-ī, culpāt-um (1), to blame
curr-us, -ūs, *m.* a chariot
custōdi-ō, custōdī-re, custōdīv-ī, custōdīt-um (4), to guard

Diān-a, -ae, *f.* Diana (a goddess)
doce-ō, docē-re, docu-ī, doct-um (2), to teach
dōn-um, -ī, *n.* a gift

95

dormi - ō, dormī - re, dormīv - ī, dormīt-um (4), to sleep

dūc-ō, dūcere, dūx-ī, duct-um (3), to lead

dulc-is, dulc-e, *adj.* sweet (like trīstis)

dūr-us, -a, -um, *adj.* hard

epistul-a, -ae, *f.* a letter

ērudi-ō, ērudī-re, ērudī-vī, ērudīt-um (4), to instruct

et, *conj.* and

exercit-us, -ūs, *m.* an army

fact-um, -ī, *n.* a deed

fēmin-a, -ae, *f.* a woman

fīli-us, fīlī or **filiī,** *m.* a son

flūmen, flūmin-is, *n.* a river

flūct-us, -ūs, *m.* a wave

fort-is, fort-e, *adj.* brave (like trīstis)

frang-ō, frangere, frēg-ī, frāct-um (3), to break

Gai-us, -ī, *m.* Gaius (a name)

Gall-us, -ī, *m.* a Gaul

ger-ō, gerere, gess-ī, gest-um (3), to carry on

gladi-us, -ī, *m.* a sword

grav-is, grav-e, *adj.* heavy (like trīstis)

habe-ō, habē-re, habu-ī, habit-um (2), to have

hast-a, -ae, *f.* a spear

hōr-a, -ae, *f.* an hour

host-is, -is, *c.* an enemy

ignāv-us, -a, -um, *adj.* idle

impedi-ō, impedī-re, impedīv-ī, impedīt-um (4), to hinder

imperāt-or, -ōris, *m.* a general

ingēns, ingentis, *adj.* vast

īnsul-a, -ae, *f.* an island

īr-a, -ae, *f.* anger

Ītali-a, -ae, *f.* Italy

iūcund-us, -a, -um, *adj.* pleasant

Iūli-a, -ae, *f.* Julia

lapis, lapid-is, *m.* a stone

laud-ō, laudā-re, laudā-vī, laudāt-um (1), to praise

Lentul-us, -ī, Lentulus (a name)

leō, leōn-is, *m.* a lion

lēx, lēg-is, *f.* a law

liber, libr-ī, *m.* a book

long-us, -a, -um, *adj.* long

lup-us, -ī, *m.* a wolf

magn-us, -a, -um, *adj.* great

mane-ō, manē-re, māns-ī, māns-um (2), to remain

man-us, -ūs, *f.* hand

mar-e, mar-is, *n.* a sea

melior, melius, meliōr-is, *adj.* better (compar. of bonus)

mēns-a, ae, *f.* a table

me-us, me-a, me-um, *adj.* my, mine

miles, mīlit-is, *m.* a soldier

miser, miser-a, miser-um, *adj.* wretched

mitt-ō, mittere, mīs-ī, miss-um (3), to send

mōnstr-ō, mōnstrā-re, mōnstrāv-ī, mōnstrāt-um (1), to show

move-ō, movē-re, mōv-ī, mōt-um (2), to move (transitive)

mult-us, -a, -um, *adj.* much, many

mūni-ō, mūnī-re, mūnīv-ī, mūnīt-um (4), to fortify

mūr-us, -ī, *m.* a wall

nāv-is, -is, *f.* a ship

nos-ter, nos-tra, nos-trum, *adj.* our, ours

numquam, *adv.* never

nūnti-ō, nūntiā-re, nūntiāv-ī, nūntiāt-um (1), to announce, declare

nūnti-us, -ī, *m.* a messenger

occīd-ō, occīdere, occīd-ī, occīs-um (3), to kill, slay

omn-is, omn-e, *adj.* all (like trīstis)

onus, oner-is, *n.* a burden
oppid-um, -ī, *n.* a town
oppugn-ō, oppugnā-re, oppugnāv-ī, oppugnāt-um (1), to attack, assault
opus, oper-is, *n.* a work

par-ō, parā-re, parāv-ī, parāt-um (1), to prepare
parv-us, -a, -um, *adj.* small, little
pater, patr-is, *m.* father
patri-a, -ae, *f.* country, fatherland
pauc-ī, -ae, -a, *adj.* few
perīcul-um, -ī, *n.* a danger
pisc-is, -is, *m.* a fish
port-a, -ae, *f.* a gate
port-ō, portā-re, portāv-ī, portāt-um (1), to carry
prīmus, -a, -um, *adj.* first
proxim-us, -a, -um, *adj.* next
puell-a, -ae, *f.* a girl
pugn-ō, pugnā-re, pugnāv-ī, pugnāt-um (1), to fight
pulcher, pulchr-a, pulchr-um, *adj.* beautiful
pūnī-ō, pūnī-re, pūnīv-ī, pūnīt-um (4), to punish

quis (*n.s.m.*), who?

rēgin-a, -ae, *f.* a queen
rēx, rēg-is, *m.* a king
rog-ō, rogā-re, rogāv-ī, rogāt-um (1), to ask
Rōma, ae, *f.* Rome

rot-a, -ae, *f.* a wheel

sagitt-a, -ae, *f.* an arrow
salt-ō, saltā-re, saltāv-ī, saltāt-um (1), to dance
sapiēns, sapient-is, *adj.* wise (like **ingēns**)
sci-ō, scīre, scīv-ī (4), to know
scrīb-ō, scrībere, scrīps-ī, scrīpt-um (3), to write

secund-us, -a, -um, *adj.* second
sede-ō, sedē-re, sēd-ī, sess-um (2), to sit
serv-us, -ī, *m.* a slave
silv-a, -ae, *f.* a wood, forest
soror, sorōr-is, *f.* a sister

tēl-um, -ī, *n.* a dart (missile), weapon
templ-um, -ī, *n.* a temple
tene-ō, tenē-re, tenu-ī, tent-um (2), to hold
terr-a, -ae, *f.* a land
terre-ō, terrē-re, terru-ī, territ-um (2), to frighten
time-ō, timē-re, timu-ī (2), to fear
timid-us, -a, -um, *adj.* timid
trīst-is, trīst-e, *adj.* sad, sorrowful
turr-is, turr-is, *f.* a tower
tu-us, tu-a, tu-um, *adj.* thy, thine, your, yours

urbs, urb-is, *f.* a city
ūtil-is, ūtil-e, *adj.* useful (like **trīstis**)

vēlōx, vēlōc-is, *adj.* swift (like **fēlīx**)
vent-us, -ī, *m.* wind
verb-um, -ī, *n.* a word
ves-ter, -tra, -trum, *adj.* your, yours
vide-ō, vidē-re, vīd-ī, vīs-um (2), to see
vinc-ō, vincere, vīc-ī, vict-um (3), to conquer
vīt-ō, vītā-re, vītāv-ī, vītāt-um (1), to avoid
voc-ō, vocā-re, vocāv-ī, vocāt-um (1), to call
vol-ō, volā-re, volāv-ī, volāt-um (1), to fly
vōx, vōc-is, *f.* a voice
vulner-ō, vulnerā-re, vulnerāv-ī, vulnerāt-um (1), to wound

ENGLISH-LATIN

all, **omn-is, omn-e,** *adj.* (like **trĭstis**)

and, **et,** *conj.*

anger, **ĭr-a, -ae,** *f.*

announce (to), **nŭntĭ-ō, nŭntĭā-re, nŭntĭāv-ī, nŭntĭāt-um,** *v.* (1)

army, **exercĭt-us, -ūs,** *m.*

arrow, **sagitt-a, -ae,** f.

ask (to), **rog-ō, rogā-re, rogāv-ī, rogāt-um,** *v.* (1)

attack (to), **oppugn-ō, oppugnā-re, oppugnāv-ī, oppugnāt-um,** *v.* (1)

avoid (to), **vīt-ō, vītā-re, vītāv-ī, vītāt-um,** *v.* (1)

beautiful, **pulcher, pulchr-a, pulchr-um,** *adj.*

bed, **cubīl-e, -is,** *n.*

better, **melior, melius, meliōr-is,** *adj.* (comparative of **bonus**)

bird, **av-is, -is,** *f.*

blame (to), **culp-ō, culpā-re, culpāvī, culpāt-um,** *v.* (1)

bold, **audāx, audāc-is,** *adj.* (like **fēlix**)

book, **liber, libr-ī,** *m.*

bow, **arc-us, -ūs,** *m.*

brave, **fort-is, fort-e,** *adj.* (like **trĭstis**)

break (to), **frang-ō, frangere, frēg-ī, frāct-um,** *v.* (3)

Britain, **Britanni-a, -ae,** *f.*

build (to), **aedific-ō, aedificā-re, aedificāv-ī, aedificāt-um,** *v.* (1)

burden, **onus, oner-is,** *n.*

Caesar, **Caesar, Caesar-is,** *m.*

call (to), **voc-ō, vocā-re, vocā-vī, vocāt-um,** *v.* (1)

captive, **captīv-us, -ī,** *m.*

carry (to), **port-ō, portā-re, portāv-ī, portāt-um,** *v.* (1)

carry on (to), **ger-ō, gerere, gess-ī, gest-um,** *v.* (3)

cause, **caus-a, -ae,** *f.*

chariot, **curr-us, -ūs,** *m.*

citizen, **cīv-is, -is,** *c.*

city, **urbs, urb-is,** *f.*

conquer (to), **vinc-ō, vincere, vīc-ī, vict-um,** *v.* (3)

country, **patri-a, -ae,** *f.*

dance (to), **salt-ō, saltā-re, saltāv-ī, saltāt-um,** *v.* (1)

danger, **perīcul-um, -ī,** *n.*

dart, **tēl-um, -ī,** *n.*

dear, **cār-us, -a, -um,** *adj.*

declare (to), **nŭntĭ-ō, nŭntĭā-re, nŭntĭā-vī, nŭntĭāt-um,** *v.* (1)

deed, **fact-um, -ī,** *n.*

deep, **alt-us, -a, -um,** *adj.*

Diana, **Diān-a, -ae,** *f.*

enemy, **host-is, -is,** *c.*

father, **pater, patr-is,** *m.*

fear (to), **time-ō, timē-re, timu-ī,** *v.* (2)

few, **pauc-ī, -ae, -a,** *adj.*

field, **ager, agr-ī,** *m.*

fight (to), **pugn-ō, pugnā-re, pugnāv-ī, pugnāt-um,** *v.* (1)

first, **prīm-us, -a, -um,** *adj.*

fish, **pisc-is, -is,** *m.*

fly (to), **vol-ō, volā-re, volāv-ī, volāt-um,** *v.* (1)

forest, **sil-va, -ae,** *f.*

fortify (to), **mūni-ō, mūnī-re, mūnīv-ī, mūnīt-um,** *v.* (4)

friend, amic-us, -ī, *m.*
frighten (to), terre-ō, terrē-re, terru-ī, territ-um, *v.* (2)

Gaius, Gai-us, -ī, *m.*
gate, port-a, -ae, *f.*
Gaul (a), Gall-us, -ī, *m.*
general, imperāt-or, -ōris, *m.*
gift, dōn-um, -ī, *n.*
girl, puell-a, -ae, *f.*
great, magn-us, -a, -um, *adj.*
guard, custōdi-ō, custōdī-re, custōdīv-ī, custōdīt-um, *v.* (4)

hand, man-us, -ūs, *f.*
hard, dūr-us, -a, -um, *adj.*
have (to), habe-ō, habē-re, habu-ī, habit-um, *v.* (2)
heavy, grav-is, grav-e, *adj.* (like trīstis)
hide (to), cēl-ō, cēlā-re, cēlāv-ī, cēlāt-um, *v.* (1)
high, alt-us, -a, -um, *adj.*
hinder, impedi-ō, impedī-re, impedīv-ī, impedīt-um, *v.* (4)
hold, tene-ō, tenē-re, tenu-ī, *v.* (2)
hour, hōr-a, -ae, *f.*

idle, ignāv-us, -a, -um, *adj.*
instruct (to), ērudi-ō, ērudī-re, ērudīv-ī, ērudīt-um, *v.* (4)
island, īnsul-a, -ae, *f.*
Italy, Ītali-a, -ae, *f.*

Julia, Iūli-a, -ae, *f.*

kill (to), occīd-ō, occīdere, occīd-ī, occīs-um, *v.* (3)
king, rēx, rēg-is, *m.*
know (to), sci-ō, scī-re, scīv-ī, *v.* (4)

land, terr-a, -ae, *f.*
law, lēx, lēg-is, *f.*
lead (to), dūc-ō, dūcere, dūx-ī, duct-um, *v.* (3)
Lentulus, Lentul-us, -ī, *m.*
letter, epistul-a, -ae, *f.*

lion, leō, leōn-is, *m.*
little, parv-us, -a, -um, *adj.*
long, long-us, -a, -um, *adj.*

many, mult-us, -a, -um, *adj.*
march (to), contend-ō, contendere, contend-ī, content-um, *v.* (3)
messenger, nūnti-us, -ī, *m.*
move (to), (trans.), move-ō, movē-re, mōv-ī, mōt-um, *v.* (2)
my, mine, me-us, -a, -um, *possessive adj.*

never, numquam, *adv.*
next, proxim-us, -a, -um, *adj.*

our, nos-ter, -tra, -trum, *possessive adj.*

pleasant, iūcund-us, -a, -um, *adj.*
praise (to), laud-ō, laudā-re, laudāv-ī, laudāt-um, *v.* (1)
prepare (to), par-ō, parā-re, parāv-ī, parāt-um, *v.* (1)
punish (to), pūni-ō, pūnī-re, pūnīv-ī, pūnīt-um, *v.* (4)

queen, rēgīn-a, -ae, *f.*

remain (to), mane-ō, manē-re, māns-ī, māns-um, *v.* (2)
Rhine, Rhēn-us, -ī, *m.*
river, flūmen, flūmin-is, *n.*
Rome, Rōm-a, -ae, *f.*

sad, trīst-is, trīst-e, *adj.*
sea, mar-e, -is, *n.*
second, secund-us, -a, -um, *adj.*
see (to), vide-ō, vidē-re, vīd-ī, vīs-um, *v.* (2)
send (to), mitt-ō, mittere, mīs-ī, miss-um, *v.* (3)
ship, nāv-is, -is, *f.*
short, brev-is, brev-e, *adj.* (like trīstis)
show (to), mōnstr-ō, mōnstrā-re, mōnstrāv-ī, mōnstrāt-um, *v.* (1)

shut (to), **claud-ō, claudere, claus-ī, claus-um,** *v.* (3),

sick, **aeger, aegr-a, aegr-um,** *adj.*

sing (to), **cant-ō, cantā-re, cantāv-ī, cantāt-um,** *v.* (1)

sister, **soror, sorōr-is,** *f.*

sit (to), **sede-ō, sedē-re, sēd-ī, sess-um,** *v.* (2)

slave, **serv-us, -ī,** *m.*

slay (to), **occīd-ō, occīdere, occīd-ī, occīs-um,** *v.* (3)

sleep (to), **dormi-ō, dormī-re, dormīv-ī, dormīt-um,** *v.* (4)

small, **parv-us, -a, -um,** *adj.*

soldier, **mīles, mīlit-is,** *m.*

son, **fīlius, fīlī** or **fīliī,** *m.*

song, **carmen, carmin-is,** *n.*

sorrowful, **trīst-is, trīst-e,** *adj.*

spear, **hast-a, -ae,** *f.*

stone, **lapis, lapid-is,** *m.*

sweet, **dulc-is, dulc-e,** *adj.* (like **trīstis**)

swift, **vēlōx, vēlōc-is,** *adj.* (like **fēlix**)

sword, **gladi-us, -ī,** *m.*

table, **mēns-a, -ae,** *f.*

teach (to), **doce-ō, docē-re, docu-ī, doct-um,** *v.* (2)

temple, **templ-um, -ī,** *n.*

tender, **tener, -a, -um,** *adj.*

thy, thine, **tu-us, -a, -um,** *possessive adj.*

timid, **timid-us, -a, -um,** *adj.*

tower, **turr-is, -is,** *f.*

town, **oppid-um, -ī,** *n.*

useful, **ūtil-is, ūtil-e,** *adj.* (like **trīstis**)

vast, **ingēns, ingentis,** *adj.*

voice, **vōx, vōc-is,** *f.*

wall, **mūr-us, -ī,** *m.*

water, **aqu-a, -ae,** *f.*

wave, **flūct-us, -ūs,** *m.*

wheel, **rot-a, -ae,** *f.*

who? **quis**

wind, **vent-us, -ī,** *m.*

wise, **sapiēns, sapiēnt-is,** *adj.* (like **ingēns**)

wolf, **lup-us, -ī,** *m.*

woman, **fēmin-a, -ae,** *f.*

wood (a), **silv-a, -ae,** *f.*

word, **verb-um, -ī,** *n.*

work, **opus, oper-is,** *n.*

wound (to), **vulner-ō, vulnerā-re, vulnerāv-ī, vulnerāt-um,** *v.* (1)

wretched, **miser, -a, -um,** *adj.*

write (to), **scrīb-ō, scrībere, scrīps-ī, scrīpt-um,** *v.* (3)

year, **ann-us, -ī,** *m.*

your, **tu-us, -a, -um** (when speaking to one person): **ves-ter, -tra, -trum** (when speaking to more than one)

SUMMARY OF RULES

1. The Verb must agree in Person with its Subject (p. 16).

2. The Subject of the Sentence is in the Nominative Case, and the Verb must agree in Number with its Subject (p. 18).

3. The Object of a Transitive Verb is in the Accusative Case (p. 20).

4. When the Subject consists of more than one Noun joined by ' and,' the Verb must be plural: when the Object consists of more than one Noun joined by ' and,' both must be in the Accusative (p. 30).

5. An Adjective must be of the same Gender, Case, and Number as the Noun which it qualifies (p. 32).

6. The Genitive Case shows to whom a thing belongs (p. 38).

7. The Complement (of a Copulative Verb) agrees with the Subject (p. 48).

8. **' By ' (or ' with ') a** *Thing*—**Ablative only.**
' By ' a *Person* **or** *Animal*—**Ablative with ' ā ' or ' ab '** (p. 54).

9. A Noun is sometimes qualified by another Noun which agrees with it in Case, and is said to be in Apposition (p. 58).

10. When an Adjective describes two or more Nouns of different Genders, the Adjective agrees with the Masculine rather than with the Feminine (p. 62).

11. When an Adjective describes 'man,' 'woman,' or 'thing,' the Noun is often omitted in Latin, and the Adjective shows by its Gender whether 'man,' 'woman,' or 'thing' is meant (p. 64).

12. 'With,' when it means 'together with,' or 'in company with,' is translated by '**cum**' followed by the Ablative (p. 66).

13. **'To,' without motion towards—Dative only.**
'To,' with motion towards—'ad' with Accusative. (p 68).

14. **Time 'when' is expressed by the Ablative.**
Time 'for how long' is expressed by the Accusative (p. 72).

15. Two Nouns joined by '**quam**' (than) must be in the same case (p. 78).

Bruce Saja
Trinity College
Cambridge.

30/9/67

D7 New Court